T0208539

THE JOURNEY BACK:
A REFLECTIVE DEVOTIONAL

WILLIAM LAYTON NELSON

authorHOUSE

AuthorHouse™
1663 Liberty Drive
Bloomington, IN 47403
www.authorhouse.com
Phone: 833-262-8899

Published by AuthorHouse 12/03/2021

ISBN: 978-1-6655-4261-6 (sc)
ISBN: 978-1-6655-4259-3 (hc)
ISBN: 978-1-6655-4260-9 (e)

Library of Congress Control Number: 2021922121

Print information available on the last page.

CONTENTS

ACKNOWLEDGEMENT & SINCERE THANKS

First, above anyone else, I want to thank God for giving me this assignment, and for His Holy Spirit who guided me every step of the way. I'm in gratitude to my family; especially my dear wife Emmeline, who tolerated me for not paying much attention during these last three months, and for disturbing her sleep as I work in the wee hours of the morning. This could not have been easy for her, but she was graciously tolerant. I also want to sincerely thank everyone for their prayers and encouraging words on continued blessings of our ministry.

What of this book, *The Journey Back*? Neither its title nor its contents really tell the full I wanted to convey to you. Let's face it, if everything were to be documented it would have taken several thousands of pages. It has been narrowed down; therefore, only small portions were extracted and written within these pages. Of course, our intention is to establish a universal caption about journeying back into the capsule of time. I encourage you to draw from the source of your own experiences; what you have had in your own lives and compare them with those within these pages. Go ahead; it's all right to put yourself in any of these stories. Go for it!

I wrote this devotional, *The Journey Back*, shortly after discussing some dreams I had with my wife Emmeline. For a few years, I have been sharing with her the dreams of my childhood, to which she stated that it might be a good idea to write a story about them. Well, she did not have to say it twice, I was interested and the very next morning I began writing. I am hoping that those who read the reflections in this devotional, especially our younger readers, will indeed find help in dealing with present and future challenges.

Every year it does not matter where in the world they are, thousands of people return to their homelands. Looking at Jacob's case, recorded in Genesis 32:24-25, the journey back was not altogether a smooth one. It was not just a dream; it was also Jacob's reality! Journeys in our imagination are so vastly different from those taken. For start, in our imagination, the journey is perfect; however, in real life, there is so much not accounted for, and many things can go wrong along the way. Nevertheless, the kind of journey I will address in this book is the type that happens in our dreams. We often dream of the past because mostly we wish we could return to change the events. However, not being physically able to journey back to those things of the past is sometimes frustrating, and even heartrending. Some dreams even leave us crying after we have awakened from fitful sleep. Because things are not the way you would have liked them to be, we are left in a disheartening predicament. It doesn't profit us to despair about the things we cannot change; instead, we should exercise faith in God to help us improve our present circumstances.

Keep on working, praying, and hoping for the best. I am wishing that all who read these pages, will not allow failures of the past to stop them from following their dreams into the future. These stories are based upon facts and honest opinions; they are spiritually inclined to lift the soul.

The Journey Back started it all; therefore, I am hoping you will agree with me that it is fitting to allow this story to be the first one in this book. I also want to take this time to thank you for allowing me to share these thoughts with you. Each of these reflections are of equal importance in this book. They are about people, things, events and places. My desire, dear reader, is for you to be encouraged as you strive to have a closer walk with our supreme Master, Jesus Christ.

DAY 01

The Recurring Dream: Journey Back in Time

God, grant me the serenity to accept the things I cannot change, courage to change the things I can, and wisdom to know the difference Reinhold Niebuhr

Have you ever found yourself returning to places you have been, sometimes in dreams and other times in reality? Over the years I have had many dreams about my past. I have noticed that the more I advance in age, the more intensified they are. So intensified, I'm involved in working in the neighborhood alongside familiar faces. Then I'd wake up exhausted but cheerful. Looking back, I realize the familiar faces in the dream were those of the past who are already deceased. These dreams occurred at least once per week. If those dreams were real, it would have been great indeed! Unfortunately, they are not.

I don't fully understand neither can I explain why I am having them. Lately I find myself thinking about a dream I had some time ago. It took me back to where we once lived in Springfield, after moving from a farm in the country. However, in the dream, people gathered in a village located between Sterling Hill and Barry Road, in St James, Jamaica. The atmosphere was friendly and casual. I lived with my parents and siblings, and the house was our residence as well as our place of business. Our father was a tailor and his sewing room was our front porch!

Let us go back to my dream. Well, there we were, standing on the side of the road. There were no chairs or benches, so people sat on rocks. Some sat on the ground as well. I'm unable to recall the details of the discussion, but I remember the faces of several of the folks present. It's amazing how one can have such vivid images of the past without even leaving the comfort of one's bed! I can even describe to you what some of the folks were wearing too!

Practically all the adults I knew when I was eleven, are now resting in their graves. Two of my brothers and a sister have also passed away. We are decades into the future from then, but the memories took me back to those days and I paused to wonder what has happened to the children of the families of the neighborhood, and where they are? Between the neighbors, there were at least thirty children! Maybe eight or so still lives in the village. The rest of us are scattered over several islands, countries, and continents of the world. Except for one neighbor who showed open disgust towards us, we all lived peacefully with each other.

Whenever I think about this recurring dream, I'm always confronted with a series of nagging questions:

Were my family and I able to attract our neighbors to Christ?

Were they able to see Jesus Christ manifested in our daily encounter with them?

On a materialistic level, my answer would be yes. As a tailor and a dressmaker, both my father and mother donated the clothes they made to others who were less fortunate. They were loving, kind and God-fearing people who reached out to others.

I also wondered if as a child I managed to impress Christ on the hearts of my young friends. We were friendly the best way we knew how, but did we do enough to encourage them to have a closer encounter with Jesus? Looking back, I knew there were few things I did not compromise, such as not eating certain types of food or doing certain things on the Sabbath. But I cannot recall talking to my friends about Jesus or if I had invited them to church! With regards to such, I failed miserably.

Nevertheless, as my thoughts journeyed back to my days of childhood, there is a cloud of gratitude for the kind of friendship we formed. As we bonded, we visited each other's homes and had several sleepovers. And while we didn't share the same Christian beliefs, we enjoyed eating and playing together. Childhood sweethearts were even formed out of some of these friendships, although there is no trace of them now. What happened?

You may ask why worry about past relationships, but we should remember that the key to our present existence is to come to terms with the past. There is no blame to go around here; life happens and sometimes relationships erode into the sandy desert of time. I believe it is due to misunderstanding how precious time is. We did not know that the shape of the future depends upon how well we mold the present. Now that we are much older, we do. Today we are looking back at a lot of barren deserts we have left behind. They are there now, just because we did not plant meaningful and lasting seeds of friendship on the sides of the path, wherein we have journeyed. Even now, we are so busy, but just a phone call or a note can keep a friendship going. Your neighbors can be here today and gone tomorrow, so make the best of it now, especially in the light of our new norm living with covid-19.

The following quote by Etienne de Grellet is something I have come to appreciate in my later years *I shall pass this way but once; any good that I can do or any kindness I can show to any human being; let me do it now. Let me not defer nor neglect it, for I shall not pass this way again.* Indeed, we are wiser today; however, for many of us, guilt is standing shoulder to shoulder with what knowledge we possess. Let's not live in the past in guilt and regret. But instead, let's start afresh and work with what we have. A potter can always break and melt his defected pots and start all over again, or he can return to the banks of the river and gather more clay. Unfortunately, it is not so when dealing with the human-race. We are not able to physically return to our childhood; therefore, as we journey back through our thoughts, let us not waste time on those things which cannot be changed. American theologian Reinhold Niebuhr (1892-1971) puts it quite appropriately in his Serenity Prayer:

God, grant me the serenity to accept the things I cannot change,
courage to change the things I can,
and wisdom to know the difference.

While we are alive, if possible, let us show love to all humankind. I am not implying that you should turn your back on family on friends; instead let's move forward to secure the relationships we have now. Let's be wise in the way we treat each other, looking to our heavenly Father to give us wisdom in making choices, and being always ready and willing to respond to the cries of His children.

I admonish you to always strive to uproot any and every un-Christlike thought and action which may be hovering outside the door of your heart: they will surely lead to the destruction of other people's lives and yours.

Use the present time well. With loving kindness treat the present and all of God's creation well, whether it be humankind or nature, treat them with uttermost respect. Try to cultivate friends who will last throughout your lifetime: friends with whom you will be able to reminisce with. You can bring the past to life whenever you choose, but bear in mind that for most, certain opportunities only come but once throughout our entire lifetime.

In this chapter, it would be remiss of me not to mention that the greatest story ever told (the story of the Savior) began by taking a journey back into time all the way back to the Garden of Eden. It's said that we must take a walk in the past to know our history in order to understand our future. The story of the Garden of Eden gives the origin and history of mankind, and the last two chapters of Revelation reveals our future. The beauty of this revelation is that God has a Garden of Eden prepared in the New Earth. And while mankind became estranged from the first garden home God had prepared, we can now move on to our new home because He has granted us the wisdom to accept the past which we cannot change (sin) and embrace the future which we can (accepting redemption).

William Layton Nelson, November 6, 2003.

DAY 02

Friends of Long Ago

This is My commandment, that you love one another as I have loved you. [13]Greater love has no one than this, than to lay down one's life for his friends. [14]You are My friends if you do whatever I command you. (John 15:12-14, NKJV).

Love is a common topic of discussion. Love can be shared with everyone (as Christ love us all) and it can be harnessed selfishly (as some do in self-love). But let's focus on the love we share with others when we form relationships and lasting friendships. Jesus must have known that as we grow older, we would be having these longings toward past acquaintances. Most adults, if not all, in some way or another, have a longing in their hearts for those individuals we have met long, long ago. This type of longing keeps us hoping that somehow, somewhere before we die, we would see those whom we had befriended in the past. It could be a family member, a classmate, a schoolmate, a roommate, a coworker, a teacher or even a preacher. We have come a long way in materializing those dreams through technology: which has tremendously enhanced the chance of locating our friends of long ago. I am not sure if you have thought this through or not but those with that longing feeling of reuniting, find themselves searching almost every day for people they knew. In many instances we no longer know their whereabouts, yet we are living with the hope of seeing them again. Sometimes we are very successful in finding some of those folks we hope to reunite with, and others, not so successful. But while throughout this lifetime we fail to reunite, God has created a beautiful way in which we can meet again. That is, the blessed hope of resurrection when all of God's children will meet on the Sea of Glass.

In our dreams of returning to the past, sometimes there are familiar faces which tend to indicate a longing to reunite with old friends. While we cannot change past events, we can however reunite with past friends, thereby once again bringing the past alive. Within the last four months I have been extremely blessed by the Lord to meet past friends and acquaintances, in which we exchanged lengthy conversations. But not all reunions end well which causes us to hastily close those regrettable chapters and move on. I am grateful for the missing links found.

When Satan rebelled in heaven and tempted the first humans to sin, the most important link of all was broken, our link to the family of God. However, a reunification is promised through a Redeemer and one of these days God will reunite the people of this earth with other sinless worlds. I am sure that the rest of the universe is waiting with great anticipation for that sweet communion once again. Someday there will be a grand reunion with One Friend whom we have never met face to face; His Name is Jesus! I am praying that as we enter this new week, we will be encouraged to appreciate our friends and our acquaintances. We should reach out to them while we can. Treat them well because the chance we have now may be the only one! I know that due of the behavior of some friends we may have to let them go but do so in love and abundant grace; even if we think they do not deserve it, let us do what Jesus would have done. As He works on our behalf, our Old Friend is longing to be with us once again.

William Layton Nelson, May 15, 2002.

DAY 03

Angel of Death! In Channels of Blessings

---

*Behold, I stand at the door and knock. If anyone hears My
voice and opens the door, I will come in to him and dine with
him, and he with Me.* (Revelation 3: 20, NKJV).

Jesus knocks at our door of our hearts; asking us to let Him in.
Unfortunately, He is not the only one knocking.

There is someone else knocking, but unlike the patient knocking of
our Savior, this knocking is impatient.

Knock, knock!

Who is it, and what do you want?

*This is the angel of death. The breath thy Master lone thee, is due today,
and I am here to collect it.*

Knock, knock!

Death knocks every day. It is a known fact that thousands of people
die every day in the world, and recently we saw a significant increase in
the number of daily deaths due to covid-19. No one knows when and the
choice is not ours to make. Wherever we are, whatever time it is, whomever
we are, it makes no difference, death still knocks. At this point, the contract
we have with Jesus concerning the breath of life is cancelled and the breath
returns to God, our Maker. This is a heavenly recall of which age is not a
deciding factor; youthfulness cannot buy us any extra time.

At the ending of our day a personal collector will slip a note under
the door of our hearts. Then, Knock, knock, knock! Every day, except on
weekends, four undertakers come to my job to collect the death certificates
of those who have passed away during the week. A few weeks ago, one
undertaker said to me:

I can hardly wait for spring to arrive.

What makes spring so special? I asked.

Her reply: Less people die during that time of the year. They have their season you know.

She continued, Peak season is usually between November and February.

For those who are in nursing homes, you can understand that most folks you are caring for they are just waiting to go off to sleep, never to be awakened again until the Day of Judgment. We pretend to fully understand death but why do we become so disappointed when a middle-aged person passes away, and we say to ourselves and others: *Why?*

Is death any different when a young person dies? The question is on everyone's lips:

Why did he/she die so young?

This may kind of sound insensitive, but it needs to be said: *Why not?*

The scripture has made it clear enough in Romans 3: 23 (NKJV): *For all have sinned and fall short of the glory of God.* Also, in Romans 6:23 (NKJV): *For the wages of sin is death.*

Indeed, that should answer the question why the young dies also. And if that is not good enough, then let us read Romans 5:12 (NKJV):

Therefore, just as through one man sin entered the world, and death through sin, and thus death spread to all men, because all sinned.

In other words, because of sin death comes to all mankind. No one (whether young or old) is exempted; and since death is a pronunciation of the consequence of sin, mankind is destined to die.

In death, we sleep, awaiting the sound of the trumpet signaling Christ's return (1 Thessalonians 4:16, NKJV): *For the Lord Himself will descend from heaven with a shout, with the voice of an archangel, and with the trumpet of God. And the dead in Christ will rise first.* Many people are passing away and a lot without any hope of hearing the first trumpet when it shall sound. But Jesus counsels us in Romans 6:12-13 (NKJV):

Therefore, do not let sin reign in your mortal body, that you should obey it in its lusts. [13]And do not present your members as instruments of unrighteousness to sin but present yourselves to God as being alive from the dead, and your members as instruments of righteousness to God.

Knock, knock!

Do we willing surrender to the angel of death when he comes knocking? Death is generally feared by humans, mainly because we don't know what's on the other side. We tend to fear what we don't know. But

Paul admonishes that death is but a sleep and in Christ, we have nothing to fear. Therefore, he boldly faced death because he knew that mankind is destined to die.

2 Timothy 4:6 (NKJV) reiterates this: *For I am already being poured out as a drink offering, and the time of my departure is at hand.*

It's my hope for all to those reading this devotional to one day joyfully say these words when death knocks:

I have fought the good fight, I have finished the race, I have kept the faith. [8]Finally, there is laid up for me the crown of righteousness, which the Lord, the righteous Judge, will give to me on that Day, and not to me only but also to all who have loved His appearing. (2 Timothy 4:7-8, NKJV).

Are you afraid to die? We should not be if we are safely secured in the fold of the loving Shepherd. If we are not altogether there yet, then let us work toward not fearing the angel of death. If today, tonight or tomorrow, you are touched by his cold icy hands, may you go with him peacefully and without regrets. Whenever it's our time, may the angel of God gently rock you to sleep.

Death reminds us that there comes a time when we must journey back to where we came from, that is, when we were just a thought, devoid of breath and life. As those who have passed on wait for the return of their Maker, they are but a memory, a thought. But as we remember our loved ones who have died, let's also remember to embrace the hope of the resurrection.

William Layton Nelson, March 22, 2007.

DAY 04

Friends and Brothers

And Jonathan said to David, Come, let us go out into the field. So both of them went out into the field. ¹²Then Jonathan said to David: ⁻The Lord God of Israel is witness! When I have sounded out my father sometime tomorrow, or the third day, and indeed there is good toward David, and I do not send to you and tell you, ¹³may the Lord do so and much more to Jonathan. But if it pleases my father to do you evil, then I will report it to you and send you away, that you may go in safety. And the Lord be with you as He has been with my father.
(1 Samuel 20:11-13, NKJV).

David's life was at stake, and he was in an urgent situation. But notice David and Jonathan took the time to solidify their friendship. It was a friendship for life and as we learned, it went even beyond Jonathan's death. Jonathan saw that the writing was on the wall concerning his father's kingdom and that nothing could stop his friend David from becoming King. He wanted to make sure that both he and his household would be safe so here he pleaded with David, his friend who was also his brother-in-law. In 1 Samuel 20:14-15 (NKJV) he says: *And you shall not only show me the kindness of the Lord while I still live, that I may not die; ¹⁵but you shall not cut off your kindness from my house forever, no, not when the Lord has cut off every one of the enemies of David from the face of the earth.*

Almost everyone has knowledge of the bible story of Jonathan and David, and the extended friendship of their families when David, as king, took Jonathan's son into the palace, to live with the royal family. David heard the voice of his friend and ran to safety. The voices of our loved ones and friends bring joy to our ears; and as we are the family of God, so too does God delight to hear from us.

Not so long ago, I received a phone call from a dear friend and brother of mine. I have not seen him or spoken with him for several years. Due to lack of consistency, over twenty years had passed. And although we didn't lack in resources (phone connection, paper and ink, etc.), we somehow had a communication breakdown. After hearing the voice on the opposite end of the line, it took me only a few seconds to recognize who it was.

I called his name.

He was surprised when he heard me say his name.

How did you know it was me? he asked.

It was not difficult to give him an honest reply to his question. I never stopped thinking about you my brother friend, and the sound of your voice remained in my memory all this time; that is how!

Yes, the space of time now seems like yesterday; nevertheless, many years and activities have taken place. The absence of true relationship in our lives is a noticeable issue. It is something money cannot buy, and it leaves within its wake a cloud of emptiness. The truth is, after speaking with my friend and his wife, I felt as if I had taken another dose of medicine for my pain. Since the year began, I have been reconnecting with friends from long ago, including old school mates. I count myself extremely blessed by God to be able to reconnect with them.

How about you, do you get excited when you hear the voices of those you love on the other end of the line?

Do you still hear the voices of friends you knew long ago, ringing in your ear?

Are you longing to see and to touch them again?

Don't think this is out of the ordinary; it's normal. *Maslow's Theory of Needs* tells us that love and belonging score the highest on the need's hierarchy of human beings. This means everyone longs for friendship!

Christ, who is divine yet human, longs for our friendship too. Being made in His image means that we possess the same feelings as our Creator. If we can feel that way about those we love, imagine our supreme Friend and Brother! Prayer brings us in close connection with Him and joins us in communication with a Friend and Brother who listens.

Even if we are separated from our friends for many years, maybe due to misunderstandings, I believe we should try to reconcile and move on. After all, true friendship does last forever. I cannot imagine how many times Jesus forgave His disciples; and in the truest of sense, they were true friends, except for one. They were loyal and faithful to Him; for example, in the Garden of Gethsemane, Peter was ready to give up his life for Him.

Do you think Jesus will ever forget such a brave act?

Or do you think He will ever forget the woman with the Alabaster box of ointment, who washed His feet with her tears?

Think back of the day you decided to accept Jesus as your Savior, stepping out in faith and forsaking the things of the world. Do you think He has forgotten that moment? Well, He has not. He has you on His mind. It is a very comforting feeling knowing that our loving Savior is watching over us, as King David says in Psalms 145:18 (NKJV): *The Lord is near to all who call on Him, to all who call on Him in truth.*

True and sincere friends do not wait until they need something from a friend to call or connect. That was not the situation between David and his Lord. Likewise, we must not wait until we are facing trouble to call on the Lord. He said He is ever near to us. That's a great comfort! And here's a bonus point He knows our voice! It is amazing how He knows six billion people by the sound of their voice. Yes, He even calls us by our names. John 10:3, (NKJV) says, *To him the doorkeeper opens, and the sheep hear his voice; and he calls his own sheep by name and leads them out.*

Isn't that wonderful? How much more intimate can we get with a Supreme God? Do you think Jesus anticipates seeing His disciples again? Think of all those who treated Him with loving kindness while He walked on this earth; and what about us, do you think He is anxious to see us as well? I think so. Even as we are struggling with life's burdens, Jesus wants us to rest our hope in the promise He made to us in John 14: 1-3 (NKJV): *Let not your heart be troubled; you believe in God, believe also in Me. ²In My Father's house are many mansions; if it were not so, I would have told you. I go to prepare a place for you. ³And if I go and prepare a place for you, I will come again and receive you to Myself; that where I am, there you may be also.*

Although the promise was made to the disciples, it's also applied to His new friends, those who have not met Him face to face, but by faith, willingly accepted Him as Savior and Lord. I think He is just itching with excitement, to return to this earth once again. O what a day, glorious day that will be!

I am not sure if I am going to wait until I get to heaven before touching Him; if it is even to touch the hem of His robe, that will do!

O my Lord and Master, I shout with a longing in my voice: Come Lord Jesus, come! Your loved ones are working and waiting for you!

Come Lord Jesus, come!

Come and take us home!

I pray that by God's grace, you will have a pleasant day. May you always be looking and longing for your Friend and Brother, Jesus Christ.

William Layton Nelson, May 19, 2004.

DAY 05

Matrimonial Bliss!

Husbands, love your wives, just as Christ also loved the church
and gave Himself for her (Ephesians 5:25, NKJV).

I would like to touch a little on a subject which affects millions of lives. The subject is marriage.

Is getting married *really* necessary?

My personal answer would be yes, if you find yourself with the right companion.

I suggest Jesus should be at the center of it all.

For centuries, thousands of couples have been hopping onto the train of matrimonial bliss. Though we wish that everyone would have a successful relationship, it's sad to say that's not always the case. Today the world is congested with broken homes, runaway children and dissatisfied spouses. If you are expecting that it will get better in this present world, then you are hoping for a lot. As far as I can see, there is no immediate solution in sight!

For a couple to have a successful marriage, they need to establish a good relationship with God; even before they think of getting married. They must first put God at the head of the table. It is futile, making plans without including Him. Next, love and respect your spouse, striving to please your partner. Strange as it may sound, if each person thinks and act this way, then despite difficulties, all will be well. Many people think marriage is smooth sailing like rolling on a velvet rug, while others believe it's a rose garden. But it is not so all the while; sometimes there are surmounting challenges.

Many years ago, I rushed into that scared realm, believing that every step I take in that world would be sublimely tranquil, but it did not take me long to find out just how wrong I was. Marriage life, if you have a God-given partner, is a beautiful life! It is the right way for a man and a woman to begin their lives together. After all, God instituted marriage right after He created humankind and He was the first to perform a marriage ceremony on Earth! Even though Adam and Eve were two individuals, God entreated them to become one flesh. Genesis 2: 24 (NKJV) reads: *Therefore a man shall leave his father and mother and be join to his wife, and they shall become one flesh.*

The devil had other ideas; he had to do something to spoil God's plan, so he lied to dear Eve.

Ye shall not surly die, he said to her (Genesis 3:4, KNJV).

Eve believed the serpent, tasted the forbidden fruit, shared some with Adam, her husband, and so it was, they exchanged life for death! Adam and Eve fell to sin, but God extended His grace. They were disciplined of course; but not abandoned. There in the place where they sinned, He promised a Savior. And after the Savior had redeemed us, He sent the Holy Spirit. If you think about it, we were never abandoned!

Why?

Christ likens his relationship with mankind as a marriage He as the husbandman, and the church as His bride. Husbands are admonished to love their wives as Christ loves the church (Ephesians 5:25). Hence, even as the church transgressed, Christ gave Himself for her and stood by her, just as husbands and wives pledge to stand by each other in sickness and in health, for better or for worse.

May God continue to bless our marriages as we reflect the example of Christ in our lives.

William Layton Nelson, April 28, 2004.

DAY 06

Macedonia Crying!

And Jesus came and spoke to them, saying, "All authority has been given to Me in heaven and on earth. 19 Go therefore and make disciples of all the nations, baptizing them in the name of the Father and of the Son and of the Holy Spirit (Matthew 28:18&19, NKJV).

Now here is the no nonsense uncompromising fact concerning the above-mentioned command.

And this gospel of the kingdom will be preached in all the world as a witness to all nations, and then the end will come (Matthew 24:14, NKJV).

I would be an extremely biased person to think that the *in all the world* meant just the place where I choose to live. It would be a tremendous strain if all who got converted to the church of our Lord Jesus Christ had to travel to Israel to worship on Wednesday nights or on Sabbaths. If every-time we want to assemble for worship or to help those in need, we end up in Jerusalem; how impractical would that be? First, we wouldn't have time for anything else. What we need to get ourselves acquainted with is the fact that whenever we receive a call to go to another area of the city, *it is a Macedonian call!* Are we willing to step out in faith in God's will, or are we just going to sit here in our seats and do nothing; what will it be?

There are times when man acts on his own intuition, and not according to God's will. Whenever we do and fail, we tend to place blame elsewhere other than ourselves. There is no personal achievement for those who want to step out in faith and try to take the word somewhere else. Whomever does is obedient to the command of Jesus Christ. The disciples were Jesus' friends, they have spent three and a half years with Him so they should have a clear sense of what He (Jesus) was talking about. What do you think would have happened if after they had established the first church, they just stayed in the building and never ventured out anywhere else?

Do you think the building would be large enough to seat two million early Seventh-day Adventists? Now there are over 12 million Seventh-day Adventist and there are other Christians as well. Would we be taking turns to schedule Sabbath worship?

There is no shame or dishonor in wanting to stay home, for some it is the best thing. Furthermore, I have no intention in taking sides with anyone who would point their fingers at you because of the decision you have made. It's your desire to serve where you are and rightly so but do not stand in the way of others who want to go to Macedonia. Everyone is on a journey through this life. My journey may take me to neglected areas in my neighborhood that need the prayers and help of church members meeting their needs; while your journey may take you to a faraway country where the gospel of Christ is presented for the first time. There are Macedonian cities and towns all over the world, and souls who are waiting to accept Jesus as their Savior. Let's not speculate on the day or week in which Jesus will return; but instead, let's labor until He comes.

By the age of twelve, Jesus was busy answering His Macedonian call and embarking on his journey. He was going about His Father's business, showing that there was no time to lose. Even before His return to heaven, He prepared the hearts of his disciples to heed the call and begin their journey, and the Holy Spirit led the way. The key is to allow the Holy Spirit to lead and guide you in that endeavor.

We should encourage others on their journey. All of us are called to be missionaries. When the hearts of God's children are stirred into action by the Holy Spirit, they should go! Obeying the command of God in this regard is like tending to a garden then watching it grow in splendor! Our job is to sow the seeds, whether it's in our communities at home or those abroad.

If you have never been involved in being a part of those who have helped to plant a branch Sabbath school or a new congregation, a Garden for the Lord, then you are surely missing out on a fulfilling feeling. Not that anything happened because of your power but just to be a partner with Jesus is joy enough! Working together as a team and doing so to help finish the work of the Lord should be our foremost concerned and not our own individual agenda. There are many avenues in which we can work for the Lord. One way is to use the talents the Lord has given to us; and when we accept our Macedonian call, He expects us to ask:

What can I do today to help others find their way to the house of the Lord?

Isaiah 6:8 (NKJV) states, *Also I heard the voice of the Lord, saying: Whom shall I send, and who will go for Us? Then I said, Here am I! Send me.*

Let's be willing to heed the call. Let's start our journey!

Do you hear the Macedonians crying?

Will you go and work for God today?

William Layton Nelson, December 2, 2002.

DAY 07

He'll Send the Rain!

*Sow for yourselves righteousness; reap steadfast love; break
up your fallow ground, for it is the time to seek the Lord,
that he may come and rain righteousness upon you.*
(Hosea 10:12, NKJV).

Have you ever found yourself up late at nights, pondering over your life, and wondering why you are where you are now? You ask the following questions:

Why am I living on this street, why this city?

Why wasn't my birth two hundred or three thousand years ago?

Why didn't it take place in another part of the world?

Lord, why am I here? Tell me, why this church? Why this congregation?

And I would like to know, why are they asking me to serve in the church?

My friends, there are souls waiting to be fed, that is why!

While it's good to reflect on our lives, it's important to know where we're going. Our journey involves fulfilling life's purposes. The fields are plowed, waiting for sowers to scatter the seeds. Let us press forward in our duties.

The Lord will ask:

What are those you have in your hands?

They are the seeds of truth, light and life!

Do not worry about the dry and hard ground; instead, do your part and leave the rest to the Lord, He will send the rain.

My toes, well they are unique, and every now and then, my wife Emmeline would ask me:

From whom, did you get your toes; was it from your mother or from your father?

Always, I laugh within me, but smile outwardly as I would think about the answer and reply as always:

Neither of them. I got them from God; these are *my* toes!

That does not go over too well with her, but she let it be until the next time the subject comes up again. For more than forty years I did not like most of me, my body, that is. My stuttering tongue included. I was not satisfied with what I got from God. I spent all those years in the *Whimsy* University, without accomplishing anything of value. If all one does at the university of life is to fill the mind with *Whimsicology*, then the more important things of life will certainly pass you by. Whimsy University does not have spiritual growth or thankfulness in its curriculum. The most liked subject, and you can get that every period, is murmuring. Yes, almost everyone signed up for that class!

However, instead of murmuring about what should or could have been, let's forget about those negative thoughts and praise God that we are wonderfully and fearfully made (Psalm 139:14, NKJV). I have discovered that learning to love and to appreciate the body God gave me is also the wonderful work of the Holy Spirit. It's the beginning of moving forward. What if we could just take away the letter Y, from the word why and turn the word into *what* or *where*? Then with eager heart, we can ask instead:

Lord, now that I am here, WHAT will you have me do?

WHAT is your mission for me?

WHERE do you want me to go?

Listen for His voice, and when He gives you the answer, go and do!

Then, He'll send the rain. He will send the Holy Spirit to work on the hearts of the men, women and children we labor for. Let us mobilize for a just and worthy cause. Let us serve our Master and the priceless souls He redeemed. There is a famine in the world for the word of God. It's in our cities and neighborhoods. There is still time for us to respond to the call.

Sow for yourselves righteousness; reap steadfast love; break up your fallow ground, for it is the time to seek the Lord, that he may come and rain righteousness upon you. (Hosea 10:12, NKJV).

Whom will I send?

Here I am Lord. Send me!

William Layton Nelson, April 21, 2004.

DAY 08

Earth's Darkest Saturday

---

*Now it was the Preparation Day of the Passover, and about the sixth
hour. And he said to the Jews, "Behold your King! ¹⁵But they cried
out, "Away with Him, away with Him! Crucify Him! Pilate said to
them, "Shall I crucify your King? The chief priests answered, "We have
no king but Caesar! ¹⁶Then he delivered Him to them to be crucified.
So, they took Jesus and led Him away.* (John 19: 14-16, NKJV).

The beauty of the past, is that it's reflective. We can look back and learn
much from it, even if we were not present at the event. The beauty of
the Scriptures is that it reveals prophecies which are detailed and can be
referenced in later books when they are fulfilled. We see this, for example,
in the life, death and resurrection of Christ. When the Jews cried: Crucify
him! they were indeed fulfilling Isaiah's prophetic message of a slain
Messiah:

He was oppressed and afflicted,
yet he did not open his mouth;
he was led like a lamb to the slaughter,
and as a sheep before its shearers is silent,
so he did not open his mouth. (Isaiah 53:7, NKJV).

Prophecies were fulfilling, right before their eyes, down to the smallest
detail, yet they refused to acknowledge it! Long before our Savior was
born, the prophet Isaiah spoke about a Messiah who would come to save
His people through His death! His own people were cheering as they led
Him away to be slain!

Lately, I've been reflective. I've been thinking about what took place,
on that special weekend, over two thousand years ago. This world was
plunged into total darkness for a while. I am not just talking about that
Friday, at the six to the ninth hour when mysteriously a dark cloud rolled

across the sky like a giant scroll, blocking out the sun. Instead, I'm referring to the hours after sunset when the Son of man rested in a borrowed tomb; and the whole universe waited, just to see what would happen next. I am sure it was not business as usual. I'm sure it must have been the darkest day in the history of the universe.

Why?

By the very appearance of the events, those who hoped in Him were sorely disappointed when He hung His head and died on the cross. Their dreams of a Messiah lifting Israel out of Roman rule, were most likely dashed when they laid him in the tomb. How could the Messiah, sent from God, the good Galilean who helped tens of thousands of people, be put to death? Jesus Christ, the one who was supposed to be the Redeemer, was mocked, shamefully hung on a tree and died. He slept in a tomb! To add to the drama of the day, the sacred veil in the temple at Jerusalem, tore in two from top to bottom in a great earthquake. *Then, behold, the veil of the temple was torn in two from top to bottom; and the earth quaked, and the rocks were split.* (Matthew 27: 51, NKJV).

The scribe who was on watch at the temple must have gotten word to the high priest concerning its destruction. Was he able to see the Most Holy Place and the Ark of the Covenant, and yet live? The place of atonement has been damaged? How can that be? Both the scribe and high priest knew the scriptures, did they begin to wonder about the things Jesus said when He was alive? Did they realize, in the early hours of the morning after a night of fitful sleep, that Isaiah's Messianic prophecies were fulfilled in their lifetime?

During the period of the Holy Sabbath hours, they should have remembered how Jesus proclaimed to Martha: *I am the resurrection and the life. He who believes in Me, though he may die, he shall live.* (John 11:25, NKJV). Sobering thoughts indeed for anyone who paid attention to the Teacher's words when He was alive. While some mocked and celebrated, others were gripped with fear; but the Savior of the world slept peacefully in His borrowed tomb among birds and butterfly cocoons.

As God the Father grieved the death of His only begotten Son, Jerusalem was in darkness and chaos. Many were filled with fear, despair, anxiety and anguish. For over thirty hours, salvation and hope were resting in a sealed sepulcher! I'm sure that night some of his followers couldn't hide their disappointment. They must have murmured and were deeply concerned about their future. They had given up all they had to follow the Rabbi, but now He was lying in a tomb.

Many probably wondered, *what's next?* Then others probably thought that He could perform a miracle to escape His predicament.

They must have discussed amongst themselves: We have seen Him perform hundreds of miracles; surely He will not allow them to kill Him. No one can kill our Master!

I believe they had thought Jesus would be released from His captors and be free. Their anticipation turned into hours of waiting to only face crushed hopes and dreams when the soldiers drove the nails into His hands.

Now the obvious questions hung in the air: *Will this man who claim to be the Son of the God of the universe; really live again?*

Will He rise on the third day, as He said He would?

With these kinds of questions, how could anyone rest peacefully that weekend? As for the disciples, they were told several times by their Master, what would take place, even as they were departing for Jerusalem, for the Last Supper in Luke 18: 31-33 (NKJV):

Then He took the twelve aside and said to them, "Behold, we are going up to Jerusalem, and all things that are written by the prophets concerning the Son of Man will be accomplished. [32]For He will be delivered to the Gentiles and will be mocked and insulted and spit upon. [33]They will scourge Him and kill Him. And the third day He will rise again

No one on earth at that time was sure what would happen next. Certainly not His disciples, for they were hiding in a house somewhere. All seemed lost.

But He was right, in that no one took His life. He willingly laid it down!

In John 10:15 (NKJV) Jesus said: *As the Father knows Me, even so I know the Father; and I lay down My life for the sheep.*

And He took it up again!

Hope in God is never a disappointment. *Now hope does not disappoint, because the love of God has been poured out in our hearts by the Holy Spirit who was given to us.* (Romans 5:5, NKJV). He rewarded their hope and as promised, Jesus rose on the third day after those dark Holy Sabbath hours had passed. The darkest Sabbath in Earth's history gave way to a beautiful Sunday morning when Jesus rose to the command of His Father, spoken by an angel sent from heaven:

Jesus, Son of David, Wake up, Thy Father Calleth Thee!

Responding to His Father's bidding, He arose from His slumber, took off His burial clothing, got dressed and left the sepulcher.

That dark Sabbath in history yielded to the Light and Life who is our Resurrection and Redeemer. Today, when we think of the Sabbath, let's remember that dark day when his disciples and followers worshipped in somber and despair, with crushed hopes and dreams. Let's greet each Sabbath with joyful hearts because He lives again!

William Layton Nelson, April 15, 2004.

DAY 09

Cast Thy Bread Upon the Waters:

Cast your bread upon the waters, for you will find it after many days.
(Ecclesiastes 11:1, NKJV).

We hear many times Do not worry; leave your tomorrows to Me!

Many of us, at one time or another, have questioned the authenticity of those words.

What does that mean?

How is that possible? We ask, mockingly. But it means exactly what the Lord said. I don't believe He would promise something if He were not able to deliver.

Simply, He's asking us to lay hold on the arm of faith, without reservation and doubt.

Why?

Is it perhaps because God is the Great I Am, who is larger than the problems we have?

Or maybe it's because He cannot be contained in a small box or within the confines of our finite minds.

Through the simple demonstration of casting our bread upon the water, the Lord is trying to teach us an important lesson. He wants us to exercise the do and have faith in Him. Casting my bread on the waters includes everything I do in my life and the talents that have been loaned to me. As followers of Jesus, we should live unselfish lives, which is the highest highs we should strive to achieve. If we strive therefore through the grace of God to live such a life, then surely the Lord will see to it that all our needs are taken care of!

However, for us to cast our bread successfully, we cannot do so grudgingly. When was the last time you happily cast your bread upon the waters? Do not worry about taking something out of your storehouse to support the cause of God or to help the needy. Even if we move far away from where you are living now, if you should run into problems God gave us a promise that He will provide: *If the clouds are full of rain, They empty themselves upon the earth.* (Ecclesiastes 11:3, NKJV).

My friends if by the grace of God, we can give to those who are in need, let us praise God for that privilege. The word of God clearly states that we should be cheerful givers.

We cannot beat God's giving neither can it be matched because He is very generous. His example is for us to follow. When we exercise the true spirit of giving, something wonderful will take place. *Now may He who supplies seed to the sower, and bread for food, supply and multiply the seed you have sown and increase the fruits of your righteousness.* (2 Corinthians 9: 10, NKJV)

There are examples in the Bible of those who choose to do otherwise. Take for instance the fellow who decided to pull down his moderate barns and build larger ones (Luke 12:16-21, NKJV). Due to his inconsiderate heart, he was weighed and found wanting. The results were grim; he departed from the face of this earth in a hurry, and took with him his plans, hopes and dreams. He did not live to partake of his bounty.

The grace we show others is meted out to us. God takes note and He blesses, not our efforts, but the trust we place in Him. When he called us to *cast our bread upon the* waters, He's calling for a life of trust and commitment.

Trust and commitment to God is not only illustrated in our actions toward others, but it's also reflected in our mindset. For example, the widow of Zarephath had just enough flour and oil to make a small cake for herself and her son. But the man of God, Elijah, spoke God's promise and she believed enough to ˝cast her bread upon the waters and trust the God he served. Throwing caution to the wind, she first made a small cake for Elijah from the little reserves she had! She embraced faith and was rewarded! The Scriptures testified that God multiplied the flour and oil for as long as the famine lasted! (1 Kings 7:7-16). They were spared from starvation. God's promises still stand today; He will do whatsoever He said He will do. He will never forsake us: no, never! Maybe you can testify about God's faithfulness in your life. Maybe you have given your last dime or something you wanted because someone needed it more; only to experience God's grace and goodness.

Has God proven Himself to you in any way?

If your answer is yes, then, testify today of His faithfulness!

In my early years, I made it a habit to carry at least five one-dollar bills in my pocket. My job back then required carrying out several errands throughout the day. While on these errands I had the opportunity to help others; seldom a day would go by without giving away the money in my pocket!

There are some exceptions though when people abuse your kindheartedness. I remember once opening my home to a young man for a few days. After answering yes, I was surprised when he showed up the next day with, not only with his suitcase, but also with his bed! He remained with us for six months, and he almost threw me out of my own house!

Nevertheless, you may be tempted to ask, William, so why are you saying these things now, and what is the real motive behind it? Well Emmeline and I have experienced some rough patches together and God, in His abundant mercies, provided for us. He deliberately placed others in our path; that even if we tried to, we couldn't have escaped them. It is so amazing just how far a small amount of faith can take you. For example, the gas gauge may be showing empty but God through His abundant mercies and grace, allows us to continue traveling ten or twenty miles down the road. When the way seems dark and dreary; just continue praying; He will not forget you: God will make a way. I know so because I am many years and thousands of miles away from where I showed just a little pity to some folks. I can say for certain that I have reaped much more than that which I have sown.

The manifestation and the power of God's word can and will only be proven true only if we act and Cast [our] bread upon the waters. Again, I say it is true because I have been a recipient of His grace, many times over.

I know you've experienced it too. Can I have a testimony from someone out there?

Sometimes the Lord allows things to happen in our lives which only serve to draw us closer to Him, like the widow of Zarephath. I know for sure that Casting my bread upon the waters with a joyous spirit and with a blessed hope did my heart a whole lot of good, as it did hers. Trusting and relying on God is simply laying hold on the arm of faith.

William Layton Nelson, January 2, 2004.

DAY 10

Choose Life!

So when Jesus heard these things, He said to him, You still lack one thing. Sell all that you have and distribute to the poor, and you will have treasure in heaven; and come, follow Me.(Luke 18:22, NKJV).

When one comes face to face with the Savior, why is it important to choose life?

Many of us today are like the rich young ruler who turns down the invitation from the Prince of Heaven. That same Jesus, is inviting us to come and have supper with Him and His Father, but we are hesitating, why?

Those things we have in our lives; things that mean so much to us; things we cannot live without; things which takes the place of the Savior; things which one day will be melted down, and be consumed by fire; *do they worth losing our place in heaven for?*

One day this whole world will be destroyed. So today choose the Savior and choose life!

Once Jesus told a young man to sell all and follow Him. *Now it happened as He went to Jerusalem that He passed through the midst of Samaria and Galilee. ¹²Then as He entered a certain village, there met Him ten men who were lepers, who stood afar off.* (Luke 17:11-12, NKJV). Choose life, Jesus is saying.

Now picture a famous rich person in our society today and imagine his/her question to Jesus:

Good Master, you are looking at one of the richest men in the world, but I do not have eternal life. What must I do in order to inherit that?

Jesus looked on him/her with compassion and then said to him. Yes, I know, but to acquire that which you seek, you are still lacking one thing. Sell all that you have and distribute to the poor, and you will have treasure in heaven; and come, follow Me.

Imagine the wheels of opposition turning and the ensuing panic attack. The rich young man probably had the same reaction while the following words echoed in his heart:

You still lack one thing. Sell all that you have and distribute to the poor, and you will have treasure in heaven; and come, follow Me. (Luke 18:22, NKJV).

He surveyed the scruffy looking disciples who followed Jesus, their feet dusty and clothes tattered, and wondered why it would take all his riches to follow the good Teacher. He looked back at Jesus, who had not gone to the Yeshiva school of Jewish scholars; who had not a house of his own, or even own a donkey; and decided against it.

No! No!

To him, that was too high a price to pay *when he heard this, he became very sorrowful, for he was very rich.* (Luke 18:23, NKJV).

And when Jesus saw that he became very sorrowful, He said, "How hard it is for those who have riches to enter the kingdom of God! ²⁵ For it is easier for a camel to go through the eye of a needle than for a rich man to enter the kingdom of God. (Luke 18:24-25, NKJV).

The young man walked away and was never heard of again.

Jesus addressed this dilemma in another instance when the multitude was gathered around Him. He asked:

For what will it profit a man if he gains the whole world, and loses his own soul? ³⁷ Or what will a man give in exchange for his soul? (Mark 8:36-37, NKJV).

My dear friends please permit me to say this, that there is nothing; nothing in this sinful, perishable world; nothing is more valuable than a trip to heaven! If that young man had chosen to follow Jesus, he would have chosen life, plus riches beyond measure. Let us not deceive ourselves, it takes full surrendering to the will of the Master for greater things to take place in our lives, yes, that's what it takes! Take for instance, those fishermen, most of them were well off. To own a boat in those days meant you were doing well. Luke was a physician and Joseph was a Prime Minister; however, they were tremendously blessed in their decision to choose life!

That sad, yet profound story of the rich young ruler is included in the Scriptures as a lesson to remind us that nothing should stand between us and the Savior. Is there something in your life that is causing you not to accept the Savior's invitation to follow Him all the way? If so, then let us unload them and choose Him. Choose life!

So He said to them, ˈAssuredly, I say to you, there is no one who has left house or parents or brothers or wife or children, for the sake of the kingdom of God, ³⁰who shall not receive many times more in this present time, and in the age to come eternal life (Luke 18: 29-30, NKJV).

But wait!

Does this mean if I take my mind off all my earthly possessions and give Christ first place in my heart, that I will have much more than what I have now, and be a happier person?

I expect He'll answer accordingly:

Yes, doubtful William, my brother. Yes, my sister Martha, do not worry about the temporal food, the Bread of Life is here!

Today Jesus is saying: Draw near to Me! However, let me warn you that there is no crown without a cross. You will suffer much but I promise I will give you joy and life eternal. Choose life! Do not worry about your lovely house, about your jobs, or about friends and family who forsake you for my sake!

I have nothing except my stony heart and the talents to give to Jesus. When you calculate it, it is not how much we have to give, but what we do with what He gives us. Take for instance, the little boy with his lunch, Jesus used it to feed over five thousand men, women and children. That young man must have become extremely popular after what he did, don't you think? Another story is the one about the widow with her mite. Notice how God gladly accepted it and blessed it.

And He looked up and saw the rich putting their gifts into the treasury, ²and He saw also a certain poor widow putting in two mites. ³So He said, Truly I say to you that this poor widow has put in more than all; ⁴for all these out of their abundance have put in offerings for God, but she out of her poverty put in all the livelihood that she had. (Luke 21: 1-4, NKJV).

All those who believe in God and choose to follow Him by surrendering all to Him, will have everlasting life. Those who have gone before us exemplified humility and total surrender. The same applies to us today when we decide to choose life!

William Layton Nelson, December 29, 2003.

DAY 11

No Time for Intermission

Be sober, be vigilant; because your adversary the devil walks about like a roaring lion, seeking whom he may devour. (1 Peter 5:8, NKJV).

On January 3, 2004, we drove across the bridge to enter Irving Texas. On our way to Las Colinas Seventh-day Adventist church, we noticed cracks in the columns, and it shook while we crossed Texas State Highway 183.

A bridge connects one place to another. It can also lead to new beginnings. Christ is that bridge that connects mankind to the Heavenly Father and gives us a new beginning. However, the devil wants to sever the connection between man and God. The Scriptures warn about the devil's intensions; the Bible declares he's like an angry lion ready to deceive, divide, conquer and destroy. But unlike the bridge on Texas State Highway 183, Christ is the only solid and reliable link that connects us to new beginnings in the eternal to come.

Therefore, as we stand on the bridge that is Christ, let's not become weary, distracted or even take intermittent rests from our doing and being good. *And let us not grow weary while doing good, for in due season we shall reap if we do not lose heart.* (Galatians 6:9, NKJV).

God wants us to remain focus on things which are important to our soul's salvation. Twelve months ago, we were wondering if we would live to see this month, but here it is, it comes around once more; thanks be unto God our Father, we have survived! In looking back at difficult times in our lives we can see how sometimes life creates the moments of intermission, whether we intend to take a break or not. These moments cause us to take a break from life's problems and focus on God's goodness. However, there are times when we purposely take an intermission from serving God and wander away from Him.

If we did, how often, and how far did we go?

Did we wander off the bridge or turn around and went back the way we came?

These are open questions, but I beseech you to take them personal, answer them inwardly! Let the answer be between you and the One who sees and knows everything!

Today, right now, let this be your resolution: *By God's grace, I will not take any more intermissions or walk away from His side.*

The fact is that our Heavenly Father never takes an intermission or a vacation from watching over us. Being alive today is proof that He is forever faithful and true to His children! He covers us with His eagle's wings of righteousness, power, and great glory! There will be trials, but do not worry about facing the challenges of life.

Why?

The God whom we serve is the grand Marshall of sincerity and faithfulness. The hymn says:

Great is they faithfulness, O God my Father, there is no shadow of turning with thee; though changest not, thy compassion, they fail not; As thou hast been Thou forever wilt be.

Yes, He has safely brought us through so far, and He will continue doing so. He has drawn us to Himself for a very special purpose; yes, to be His witness.

You should know that when you decide to serve God, the devil will make you his next target. But don't be afraid of Satan flexing his muscles, God has promised to never leave nor forsake you. Therefore, while God keeps His promise, let us keep ours. Let's be steadfast in our lives and mission of service. Let's go wherever He sends us to spread the good news on the streets of Macedonia! Let's trim our lamps so that they will always burn for Jesus, because there is no time for intermission! Let's give ourselves over to the Holy Spirit that our thoughts and actions are one with His!

Until the day where there are no more tears, I pray that we will continue to be faithful to our Lord and our Master. There shouldn't be any time for intermission while we walk this pilgrim's pathway. There shouldn't be any more time out from our duty to our fellowmen. There should be no more intermissions.

William Layton Nelson, January 3, 2003.

DAY 12

Fishers of Men & Women

And Jesus, walking by the Sea of Galilee, saw two brothers, Simon
called Peter, and Andrew his brother, casting a net into the sea;
for they were fishermen. ¹⁹Then He said to them, ¯Follow Me, and
I will make you fishers of men (Matthew 4: 18-19, NKJV).

In the last three and a half years of His life, Jesus demonstrated to us several ways how to witness. He went everywhere He was needed and so should we.

For the past few years, many of us have taken up the challenge to go! I am not afraid to go, are you? We are missionaries wherever we go, whether within our own communities or abroad. Jesus calls us to go wherever we are needed. This reminds me of the lyrics of the song *I Will Make You Fishers of Men* (Written by: Harry D. Clarke, Copyright: Unknown):

Here Christ calling, come onto me,
come onto me, come onto me.
Here Christ calling, come onto me,
and I will give you rest.
I will give you rest, I will give you rest.
Here Christ calling, come onto me,
and I will give you rest.

I will make you fishers of men,
fishers of men, fishers of men.
I will make you fishers of men,
if you follow me.
If you follow me, If you follow me,
I will make you fishers of men,
If you follow me.

As I was whistling the tune while I worked, a feeling of excitement came over me. I felt a sense of gratitude and a flood of emotion as I considered that God wants to include me in His plan of salvation. I could not hold back the tears flowing down my cheeks, and I thanked Him for this marvelous opportunity to work for Him, in His vineyard. I have noticed that the last two years or so I have been slowly creeping out of my cocoon of timidity and fear in sharing His word. I am finding great joy, casting out into the deep as I embrace my duty as a fisher of men.

There should not be any shame being in a ship which is captained by Jesus Christ. But we are not in the boat to sip tea. It's fishing time! Cast out your nets into the deep. Don't be concerned about the type of water, whether it is salty or fresh, or even the type of fish. Christ has called you to fish, don't discriminate - fish is fish!

Throw out your line of hope into the sea of men and women and with loving kindness haul them into safety. We should not forget to attach some weight of understanding and compassion. Before we toss our line out into the waters, we should make sure to remove the obstacles of self-righteousness and ˜holier-than-thou attitudes. Let's humble ourselves before the Lord and He will use us in a mighty way. If you are not experiencing that inner sweetness of desire to witness, then ask God to fill your soul with longing for the salvation of souls. Ask Him to entice your appetite with the sweet-smelling flavor of missionary work. He is waiting to anoint you and make you a fisher of men. There is no better life than that of serving the Master.

When I lived in the city of Rochester, NY, I would often go fishing with my brother. I recall standing on the banks of the river, gazing into the water. There were schools of salmon slowly swimming upstream. We dropped our hooks into the water, and although it took us up to an hour, we reeled in our fish. The city limits only three fish per catch per person; but when we are in Christ's boat, there is no limit! There are thousands of souls waiting for us to bring them the good and marvelous Good News of Salvation. In their day, the disciples boldly proclaim the gospel. Pray for the power and wisdom of the Holy Spirit, then go and do likewise. *Ask, and it will be given to you; seek, and you will find; knock, and it will be opened to you.* (Matthew 7:7, NKJV).

The time is fast approaching; let us seize the opportunity now, while we can. We can only do so when we are fully committed to Him. Let us go fishing for our Master!

William Layton Nelson, November 15, 2004.

DAY 13

Physically Strong but Spiritually Weak

---

*Then Moses answered and said, "But suppose they will not
believe me or listen to my voice; suppose they say, "The Lord
has not appeared to you* (Exodus 4:1, NKJV).

The morning I decided to renew my work for the Lord, I armed myself
with some evangelistic materials, including some of my new CDs and
cassettes. The idea was to give them out to those I met on my morning
walk. However, I kept on saying to the Lord:

Lord, You know that I am physically strong but spiritually weak.

Like Moses, I sometimes stutter in speech, and I have used this as an
excuse for forty years and got pretty good at it; but that morning, I wanted
a change. On my first lap, I met a lady in the parking lot. She had just
finished strapping her little boy in the rear seat of her car when I greeted
her. She surprised me with a broad smile, as she returned the greeting. It
was then I offered her one of the packages. She politely refused my offer.
I smiled and wished her a pleasant day, and off I went.

I realized it was a simple process, but not an easy one. I went around
the bend, still feeling totally embarrassed. I heard a voice in my head:

See, you are not good at this! Look, can't you see how you have just
embarrassed yourself?

I wanted to just finish the lap, climb the stairs to our apartment; go
into my office, pull the blinds all the way down and seal it tight!

I begin questioning my intentions:

Why bother walking around with these things in my pockets and in
my hands?

My inner voice whispered, This lady turned you down. It is too
embarrassing. Surely you do not want her to see you again.

What a waste of time!

It was really getting to me, creeping up under my skin.

Yet another voice:

You have been giving away your *I Promised God* cassettes and CD's to folks so don't give up now. The *Vibrant Life* pamphlet, the *Discover Card*, *Happiness Digest* and *Steps to Christ* have brought joy to many, so keep on going. So far you have distributed almost fifty and only one individual rejected your offer; that is great!

God surely has ways to encourage those who decide to work for Him. For example, I received the following message from another lady living in the same complex.

> *Dear Mr. Nelson,*
>
> *I wanted to find a way to thank you for your tape, and your friendly smile every morning, and then I found your website on the tape cover... Your website is very awesome! Very powerful poetry.*
>
> *Thanks again for your warm smile and positive message. You have truly touched my heart, and I pray that you continue to touch others.*
>
> *Your Friendly Neighbor.*

My heart was blessed and encouraged by the note, and I have not looked back since!

I have several stories like that one, and I am sure you may have several too.

Moses spent a great deal of time arguing with the Lord about his deficiencies. I imagine being out in the field, doing all that hard work should have made him a strong man. However, he was physically fit, but spiritually weak. Think about it, this is the same Moses, who was groomed in the palace of the king. It is the same Moses, whom Pharaoh would have chosen over his own son, to succeed him on his throne. This same Moses who would have become king had the choice been made. Of course, had it not been for his own countryman revealing what he did, it would have been so.

There he was, trying to whine himself out of a mission, chosen for him by God.

Then Moses said to the Lord, ˉO my Lord, I am not eloquent, neither before nor since You have spoken to Your servant; but I am slow of speech and slow of tongue (Exodus 4:10, NKJV).

Does that sound familiar? It's familiar for me as I am also a person who stammers and of slow speech. Maybe a million times or more, I have gotten angry with myself for not saying something when I should have. Yes, it always comes after I have missed opportunities. I have been living with this impediment, but I'm determined to continue working for the Lord. My prayer is that He will give me boldness of heart to say the words I need to say for Him.

Do you sometimes feel the way Moses felt, physically fit but weak in faith?

Realizing that the Holy Spirit guides my thoughts, was the true eye-opener to my new-found boldness later. You too, all of us, can become bold when we allow the Holy Spirit to work within us, if we are only willing to lay our fears at the Master's feet. We may not be able to accomplish what Moses did, but a mission is a mission, whether great or small, the Lord rewards our faithfulness. We cannot know for certain how large a dent our small deeds will leave on our friends, neighbors, coworkers, employees, employers, and our families. However, if we diligently ask the Savior to help us to combine physical strength with the smooth working of the Holy Spirit, He will grant it to us.

I pray that this will be our goal, and for God richest blessings on you,

William Layton Nelson, October 18, 2004.

DAY 14

Consider the Fruit Flies

But the children of Israel committed a trespass regarding the accursed things,
for Achan the son of Carmi, the son of Zabdi, the son of Zerah, of the tribe
of Judah, took of the accursed things; so the anger of the Lord burned against
the children of Israel. ²Now Joshua sent men from Jericho to Ai, which
is beside Beth Aven, on the east side of Bethel, and spoke to them, saying,
'Go up and spy out the country. So, the men went up and spied out Ai.
(Joshua 7:1-2. NKJV).

Our sinful habit may not be visible to others, but God knows all about it. *Israel has sinned, and they have also transgressed My covenant which I commanded them. For they have even taken some of the accursed things and have both stolen and deceived; and they have also put it among their own stuff.* (Joshua 7:11, NKJV).

Have you ever observed fruit flies? Once there are fruits, the fruit flies will appear; and the only way to be rid of them, is to get rid of the fruits! As a matter of fact, they'll stay awhile as the smell of the fruits linger in the air. Once at work, I left a ripe banana in my desk drawer and forgot about it. Even after getting rid of the banana, it took several days before the fruit flies eventually went away.

Sin carries with it a lingering effect; and whenever we allow ourselves to become drunken with sinful habits, we tend to be swarmed and overwhelmed by its effects. God warns us in 1 Peter 5: 8 (NKJV), *Be sober, be vigilant; because your adversary the devil walks about like a roaring lion, seeking whom he may devour.*

The devil and his crew are like those fruit flies. They surround our weaknesses to keep us dwelling on them. But for the child of God, who is dwelling in God's grace, sin becomes so annoying, a nuisance.

How do the fruit flies know there are fruits nearby?

Fruit flies have been studied. Research findings indicate that by using their antennae, fruit flies have a keen sense of smell.

How does the devil know our hearts?

While he's not using his sense of smell to detect our weaknesses, he uses his observatory skills. I'm sorry to be the bearer of such disturbing news, but yes, the devil watches us keenly. It is how he detects our weaknesses. He preys on them, tapping the same vulnerabilities over and over again.

In this present life, we may have to go through troublesome times, but do not despair. If we remain faithful to Jesus, He promised in His word, He will see us through. *Behold, I am with you and will keep you wherever you go, and will bring you back to this land; for I will not leave you until I have done what I have spoken to you.* (Genesis 28:15, NKJV).

All throughout the Bible, from Genesis to Revelation, His promises can be found. He will be with us. There is no need to be afraid. David reminds us about the promise God made to all His children: *For He shall give His angels charge over you, to keep you in all your ways* (Psalm 91:11, NKJV). And Paul in Philippians 4:7 (NKJV), reminds us too that *the peace of God, which surpasses all understanding, will guard [our] hearts and minds through Christ Jesus.*

Paul took Jesus at His word, and as a result was able to write to young Timothy about the reason for his deep faith: *For this reason, I also suffer these things; nevertheless, I am not ashamed, for I know whom I have believed and am persuaded that He is able to keep what I have committed to Him until that Day.* (2 Timothy 1:12, NKJV).

When and if the fruit flies of sin assail us, if our anchor is fastened to the Rock Christ Jesus, then we have nothing to fear. With that sort of determination as that of Paul, surely the fruit flies of sin will stay away, or they will not be able to penetrate our defenses. Christians are admonished to *put on the whole armor of God, that you may be able to stand against the wiles of the devil* (Ephesians 6:11, NKJV).

And He tells us how to do it! God does not leave us unprepared. He gives us the instructions on how to stand in His might in Ephesians 6: 14-18 (NKJV):

Stand therefore, having girded your waist with truth, having put on the breastplate of righteousness,

[15]and having shod your feet with the preparation of the gospel of peace;

[16]*above all, taking the shield of faith with which you will be able to quench all the fiery darts of the wicked one.*

[17]*And take the helmet of salvation, and the sword of the Spirit, which is the word of God;*

[18]*praying always with all prayer and supplication in the Spirit, being watchful to this end with all perseverance and supplication for all the saints.*

Whatever is in our lives attracting the fruit flies of sin, let it go and armor up!

William Layton Nelson, June 10, 2007.

DAY 15

Orphans in God's House

As a child, my siblings and I were fortunate to have both parents in our lives; however, on reaching my 22nd birthday, our beloved mother passed away. Our father lived for almost 30 years after her death. For us, we've never viewed ourselves as orphans because our parents were with us in our adult lives.

But do you have to lose parents to feel orphaned?

There are many people who are orphaned by friends and family members by neglect. We see it often when people get lost within large groups like a church or a school. For example, someone can feel isolated in a large church, or even in a small church where most of the members are related. Even in churches where your ethnic background is way out numbered or where professionalism owns the pulpits.

Then sometimes we feel orphaned when our spiritual walk with God is not as it's supposed to be. Therefore, when we are amongst other believers, we feel extremely isolated. There are several instances when isolation in the household of faith is unbearable the person next to you is downright cold; and our self-esteem takes a tumble when we are treated as if we're invisible.

We should cultivate a spirit of friendliness. If all of us strive to live that way, then surely enough, we will find others reaching out to us. Some of us are bold enough to say that the church is a boring place to be, maybe so for some, but what are you doing personally to change that? The book of Lamentation is filled with orphan gripes and it describes the state of mind the children of Israel were in. *We have become orphans and waifs, our mothers are like widows.* (Lamentation 5:3, NKJV).

But what if church members pulled together with the determination ʿall for one and one for all? Then it would be difficult in our congregations to tell people apart. In the huge household of our heavenly Father and His Son Jesus Christ, there should be no orphans. From the moment we enter in through His doors and He enrobes us with His righteousness that makes us all equal. *But when the fullness of the time had come, God sent forth His Son, born of a woman, born under the law, [5]to redeem those who were under the law, that we might receive the adoption as sons.* (Galatians 4:4-5, NKJV). Even if we are treated as orphans, let us not accept that kind of treatment. Through the begotten Son of God, we are no more orphans, because in God's sight we are just as important as the person sitting next to us.

William Layton Nelson, July 1, 2004.

DAY 16

There is Still Room

Some years ago, Emmeline and I flew to Mexico City; she was there attending a conference, so I went along with her. She decided to visit the City of Puebla, where she had some batch mates and friends she knew, when she attended the University of Puebla. It took us a few hours to get there. After disembarking at the bus terminal, we took a taxi to the address we had; but it was the wrong place. We did not realize our mistake, until after the cab was gone! However, the people in the area were very friendly and they directed us to where we wanted to go. There was a slight difference with the spelling of the two streets in question; and the cab driver had made the common mistake! A store owner told us that the minibuses run frequently, and one would take us to our destination.

After waiting a few minutes, the bus came, and I looked inside. Even though it was early afternoon, inside the van was dark and crammed with people. Like a trained army, the passengers began shuffling around, and beckoned to us in Spanish.

Very soon those who were sitting made enough room so Emmeline could sit down. I was standing up; well, bending over that is, because there was no room to stand upright. As we rode, I closed my eyes and the cramped space reminded me of the old days in Jamaica. While the vans were licensed to carry a certain number of passengers, it was normal for people to sit on each other, scrunch, squeeze and whatever it takes, in order to make room for others. At night it was even more dramatic! People seldom complained, unless someone was too heavy.

Now let us look at the church which has been built on the Rock Christ Jesus. If a congregation is growing in leaps and bounds, some people are worried about losing their special place in a certain pew or a cherished office. We should not worry about the rapid inflow; you won't be crushed by the multitude. There is a lot of space on God's earth to accommodate those who accept Jesus Christ as their Lord and Savior.

Let's take note that Jesus issued the invitation and therefore when our churches overflow, it's as a result of people responding to Christ's invitation. He stated that all will be invited; all are welcomed *And this gospel of the kingdom will be preached in all the world as a witness to all the nations, and then the end will come.* (Matthew 24:14, NKJV).

Just notice what happened to Jesus after His Father congratulated Him from heaven:

Then Jesus was led up by the Spirit into the wilderness to be tempted by the devil. (Matthew 4: 1, NKJV).

Praise God, Jesus triumphed over the devil. Notice also what He did after He had His encounter with Satan:

From that time Jesus began to preach and to say, ¯Repent, for the kingdom of heaven is at hand (Matthew 4: 17, NKJV).

This should be the attitude of every child of God, sharing the coming kingdom of God with others. If we pay attention to global news, we seem to be in the days which Jesus speaks about - the kingdom of heaven *is* at hand! This is the time to make room in our church pews to accommodate the world! This is the time when we say:

There's room in the house of God for more! Jesus welcomes all!

How about your neighborhood church? Is it asleep or wide-awake proclaiming the gospel of Jesus Christ? When it comes right down to it, the Master still loves us, even though we have been ignoring Him for so long, He still cares.

We should also ask ourselves: Is there still room in my life for the Savior?

You can always make room in your life for the Savior to make a working disciple out of you. He will never turn you away. He will always welcome those eager to become true children of God. Therefore, let us determine in our hearts to make room for Him. *Let us lay aside every weight, and the sin which so easily ensnares us, and let us run with endurance the race that is set before us.* (Hebrews 12:1, NKJV).

There is still room for you to be a lighthouse in the service of the Lord. Praise God there is still room to fulfill that blessed hope. It's God our heavenly Father who establishes it, and I pray that by His grace, we will always find hope.

William Layton Nelson, November 25, 2002.

DAY 17

Through the Storm

We were on our way from Galveston Texas to our home in Dallas. We were less than 100 miles from home, and in the distance, we could see the lightning dancing. The closer we got, the more spectacular it became. The thunder roared with authority as we watched the streaks of lights danced as if moving to the sound of mighty drums. It did not take us long before we found ourselves under a darkened cloud. Visibility suddenly decreased from 3 miles to about 50 feet. Cars began pulling over to the shoulder to wait out the storm, but I kept on moving forward. I had home on my mind. Emmeline occasionally looked at me, and I knew she was concerned. I told her that if we go ahead carefully, things would be okay. I assured her if it became dangerous, then we would pull over on to the shoulder.

Despite the danger, I was hopeful. I had a feeling that somewhere up ahead the storm would be over. Somewhere up ahead the sun would be shining brightly once more. Somewhere ahead sooner, the pouring rain that penetrated the darkened cloud would stop and my vision would be clear once more. I pressed on with a prayer on my heart, believing God would take us through safely, and He did!

I felt the presence of God with us and as we drove through the storm, our hopes lifted. Soon it was possible for us to see the border where the rain cloud changed to the clear blue sky and our hearts leaped with joy! The thunderstorm was about three miles behind us when we made a pit stop. The area where we stopped was dry and a strong wind blew old bits of paper, shrub and dust all around us, just the way you see it in the western movies. The extreme weather change was unbelievable!

In many cases life's journey is just like that, where thick and darkened clouds hang over us, and our lives become so uncomfortable, so entangled and hope becomes dimmed, and we give in. Then there are other times when we pull over to the shoulder, recline our seats, lean back, close our eyes, and wait for the storm to subside. That truly works well for those who know their limitations, but sometimes the storm doesn't subside. Many of us are in the wrong place at the start of the storm and become trapped beneath the dark stormy cloud year after year, getting soaked. Sometimes all we need to do is to take a step forward in faith, that is, keep our eyes on Jesus. For those who are like me, those who are more inclined to push forward for as long as we can see a few feet in front of us, we move on.

Our natural tendency as humans is to get out and away from the storm; we want to breathe freely. But what if God sent the storm to build your faith, resilience, and hope? Everyone encounters storms, but God promised to take us through each storm, if only we hold onto Him and trust Him.

William Layton Nelson, June 5, 2001.

DAY 18

Some Dreams Lie!

I had a dream. I had returned to my village in St James. It was after I made a lot of money from my career in music (trust me I was disappointed when I realized this part was a dream). I was surprised when I got there because I was expecting to see a great deal of change in my hometown, but everything was the same; except for one house, we will get to that later.

In my dream, everyone and everything in the village were the same age as I had left them forty years ago! The Shoeblacks (Hibiscus) plants were still standing tall, forming fences, around the houses. The Barn-net-bush square, looked the same! Everyone remembered me and greeted me with hugs, pleasant smiles, and cheerful laughter. While I held on to my guitar, someone helped me with the rest of my luggage. No one there gave any indication that anything was wrong. As I left the square and headed to my grandparents' place, I noticed that one house in the village changed dramatically! The house was shabby looking and broken down. I recalled every two or three years they used to repaint it green with white trims. I was disappointed at the sight of it.

The house! I exclaimed. What happened to it, and where are the people?

Suddenly, everyone became sad. Their heads hung low, without saying a word! Some were even using the tips of their shoes to dig holes into the ground. I noticed the pain on their faces, I could almost see the tears traveling across the narrow rim of their lower eyelid; still no one spoke.

I remembered as a small boy, how we would visit that beautiful house to see my aunt and her family. Suddenly the village came to life with the occupants performing their familiar routines, such as the milkman passing by with his mule to collect the empty milk containers and the truck driver who transported the milk to the factory in Montpelier had already returned, after delivering his cargo.

But I noticed one important thing was missing. The children. Where were the children? Where were the kids I grew up with? I couldn't help but wonder anxiously. Suddenly, I wanted to hurry to my grandparents' house to see if my cousins were there. It was then, that my dream left me! My eyes opened and I looked at the clock on the dresser; it was a quarter past 3 in the morning. My dear wife was sleeping softly beside me. It was at that very moment, I realized that my dream lied to me!

Have you ever dreamt you were flying, swimming, falling from a high building or from the sky? If you have, then you know how it feels after you are awakened from your dream. I know for sure that if I remain faithful, one day I will fly, not out or down but upward to glory. Although often I have been disappointed by some of my dreams, other times I am glad they were not true. There is one dream I am looking forward to seeing it fulfilled, and that is to see Jesus coming in the clouds of glory. *When the Son of Man comes in His glory, and all the holy angels with Him, then He will sit on the throne of His glory.* (Matthew 25:31, NKJV).

For thousands, maybe millions, of people, life is a very bad dream that they'd like to wake up from. But I've realized that sometimes in our dreams, while we have nothing tangible to hold onto, we however can hold onto hope. And sometimes we are awakened from the dream, hopeful. In this life you may even see some of your dreams crumble at your feet but do not give in, keep focusing on what you are doing and where you are going. Jesus said that He would come again, believe His words and wait on Him. Despite our dreams turning out to be false or lies, hope in Christ never disappoints *Now hope does not disappoint, because the love of God has been poured out in our hearts by the Holy Spirit who was given to us.* (Romans 5:5, NKJV).

I pray that Gods richest blessings will remain with you always and forever.

William Layton Nelson, April 26, 2004.

DAY 19

I Promised God

The Lord is not slack concerning His promise, as some count slackness, but is longsuffering toward us, not willing that any should perish but that all should come to repentance.
(2 Peter 3: 9, NKJV).

Ever since I was a teenager, because of my small impediment, my will to move about stress-free is restricted. At the early stage in my life, my greatest ambition was to get rich, live comfortably and help as many people as I possible could; with the hope that I could work at my own pace, doing what I do best. Although my dream to be financially rich has not realized, I am happy and thankful for being rich in God's mercies. Now I have a burden on my heart for serving others, more than I have for things of this world. Every now and then though, I still ask the Lord to please take away those pains which causes a great deal of discomfort; after all, that would be a great relief for me.

When I celebrated my 57th birthday, my family prepared a special meal. I was very happy, as I thought about how blessed I am to experience the love of family. As I looked at the cards and the gifts, my mind raced back to the days of my childhood. I remembered the first birthday party hosted by my friend in my honor. It was great and I was appreciative. And although I was only a teenager then, I understood experiencing the riches of God. I promised Him then, and many times after, that I would be true to Him.

At the table, I could hear the voices of my family, but I could not see their faces very clearly. I was distracted, imagining myself in Rochester New York, on Alexander Street, face down on the sidewalk.

Okay, let me tell you the story from the beginning. I worked at the Hickey-Freeman clothing company in Rochester New York: One morning I was heading for the bus stop on my way to work when I became dizzy.

I struggled to keep my balance and even on reaching the bus top, I had difficulty standing straight. I thought that it was foolish of me to try to go to work, so I returned home. Afterwards, I called in sick, then called my brother's home to alert them to my condition.

Later that morning my sister-in-law Jacquelyn, visited with things I needed for the day. I met her in the parking lot, thanked her and headed back to the apartment building. However, my knees buckled beneath me, when once again the feeling returned. Like someone intoxicated I headed toward the busy street into the oncoming traffic. A light blue Buick headed toward me. I was unable to speak but I remembered calling out in my silence saying:

Lord save me!

I lost all consciousness, and in a few seconds, which seemed like eternity, I found myself face down on the ground.

By this time my pride was wounded; it was embarrassing to be caught in such an undignified manner, so I tried standing. Yes, even though I was not thinking straight, pride took center stage over everything else. I was half dazed on my hands and my knees, desperately trying to force myself up. While doing so, my sister-in-law who was about to drive away, had seen the incident and came to my assistance! Thank God the hospital where she worked was just across the street, and she took me to the emergency room. My diagnosis was dehydration.

Dehydration!

I was so afraid of dying that day. The reason?

I was not prepared.

My soul was not ready to face God. While I was there on my face, realizing that I was unable to get up, I begged God to lift me up and promised to serve Him faithfully and truthfully for the rest of my life. Just how long I was there on my face, I am not sure; but later that day I realized how desperate I was. The skin on my forehead and in the palm of my hands was missing; they were left on the sidewalk.

Seven years have passed since that scary day, yet that horrible experience is still fresh in my mind. I have promised God many times since then and I never kept my word but today I am sincere about my promises I have been making to Him since long ago. I fully understand that it is only through Him that my soul can have lasting peace. We should never make promises to God and our fellowmen just because we are in danger; instead, our promises should come from a sincere heart. I was feeling so grateful for what the Lord had done for me. He has pulled me from the jaws of death so many times!

I could not sit still any longer, so I asked to be excused from the dinner table and went to my computer; there I started writing these words:

Yes, I promised God:
When everything was going wrong, my face down to the ground.
I tried to get up from where I was, I end up hurting myself even more.
Lord it was in my desperation, I made this vow to you.
You knew my heart back then Lord, yet you saved me anyhow.

Refrain:
Yes, I promised God that if He ever lift me up,
I would serve Him until I die.
Yes, I promised God,
He gave me the will, to rise up again,
so why shouldn't I honor my word, when I promised God?

My dreams were shattered on every side, I did not see any way out.
I watched as they fulfilled with someone else,
It left me wondering what is going on.
Lord now from a sincere heart, I am making this vow to you.
I promise I would serve you. You're making my dreams come true.

May the Lord help us that as we go through life day by day, hour by hour and minute by minute. Let's ask Him to allow the Holy Spirit to help us keep the promises we make to our Savior and the people around us. Let me put it another way: As children of the Heavenly King, we should be faithful in our words, our deeds and in our actions.

Why? Because He is faithful in His!

The Lord is not slack concerning His promise, as some count slackness, but is longsuffering toward us, not willing that any should perish but that all should come to repentance. (2 Peter 3: 9, NKJV).

William Layton Nelson, March 3, 2002.

DAY 20

Who'll Be Number One?

At that time the disciples came to Jesus, saying, "Who then is greatest in the kingdom of heaven? (Matthew 18:1, NKJV).

There were heated discussions among the disciples about who would be the greatest in Christ's kingdom. Each one was in line to be number two in Jesus' kingdom, but whom? You can bet every chance they got they were trying to outdo each other or impress the Savior.

While they didn't display the attitude of the Publican in Luke 18:13, there was a quiet war raging between them. Jesus knew the danger of elevating self and how pride can affect our walk with Him. He therefore used a little boy to demonstrate the kingdom of God.

Then Jesus called a little child to Him, set him in the midst of them, ³and said, "Assuredly, I say to you, unless you are converted and become as little children, you will by no means enter the kingdom of heaven. ⁴Therefore whoever humbles himself as this little child is the greatest in the kingdom of heaven. (Matthew 18:2-4, NKJV).

A habit of the disciples was to prevent others from seeing the Savior. Thank God, salvation is not in the hands of sinful men. Mankind's need to feel important is the very opposite attitude of Christ, who *made Himself of no reputation, taking the form of a bondservant, and coming in the likeness of men* (Philippians 2:7, NKJV), to die on a cross and take our punishment instead. They saw His humility, yet they were not eager to duplicate His character in their own lives; other things were on their minds, like power!

It is interesting to see, after four thousand years we still haven't learned much in that regard, Instead, we possess the destructive I/ME disease of which we are center of our own universe. The little child sensor within us has long been obliterated, and selfishness is ruling our hearts with supreme authority! That, which we needed most to make our lives truly worth something in the Father's eyes, has been tossed out, gone!

Listen to what Jesus had to say to His disciples and to us today: *Therefore, whoever humbles himself as this little child is the greatest in the kingdom of heaven.* (Matthew 18:4, NKJV). Elevating self is not for humans to do; instead, that's according to the will of God. And He chooses to elevate humans as He sees fit according to His will and not ours.

Humble yourselves in the sight of the Lord, and He will lift you up. (James 4:10, NKJV).

One example can be found in 1Kings 3:1-28, where Solomon prayed for discernment and wisdom when he inherited the throne from his father David. He said:

Therefore, give to Your servant an understanding heart to judge Your people, that I may discern between good and evil.

For who is able to judge this great people of Yours? (1Kings 3:9, NKJV).

In humility, Solomon acknowledged that he knew nothing about ruling God's people in a way that would be pleasing to God. That's because he saw himself as sinful before this great God. Therefore, he humbled himself, and God exalted him:

The speech pleased the Lord, that Solomon had asked this thing.

[11] Then God said to him: "Because you have asked this thing, and have not asked long life for yourself, nor have asked riches for yourself, nor have asked the life of your enemies, but have asked for yourself understanding to discern justice,

[12] behold, I have done according to your words; see, I have given you a wise and understanding heart, so that there has not been anyone like you before you, nor shall any like you arise after you.

[13] And I have also given you what you have not asked: both riches and honor, so that there shall not be anyone like you among the kings all your days. (1Kings 3:10-13, NKJV).

Solomon trusted God and He did what He said He would do. Are we locking that trust in Jesus; believing that He will do what He said He would do? If we keep on telling ourselves, that we can be seen only if we personally lift ourselves up, then we are in serious trouble. In humility we need to place ourselves at the feet of Jesus so we can live according to His will for our lives.

The disciples asked to be number one, but we can never be number-one; Jesus is, and always will be. He is the begotten of the Father, remember?

My fellow Christian friends, I leave you with this thought; well, it is a question which all of us need to ask ourselves, individually and collectively.

Am I there yet?

As a body of Christ, are we living amongst one another the way we should? I do hope and pray that throughout the entire world, from every Christian's heart, these words will echo:

Look upon Jesus, sinless is He. Father impute His life unto me. (F.E. Belden, 1940).

William Layton Nelson, November 5, 2004.

DAY 21

Amazing Grace Bowed Low

And of His fullness we have all received, and grace for grace.
¹⁷For the law was given through Moses, but grace and truth
came through Jesus Christ. John 1:16-17, NKJV).

Did you know that the plan for Christ's arrival on Earth was set in motion thousands of years before the time He came? If you can recall, it was after mankind was tricked by the devil that God instituted the plan of salvation found in Genesis 3:15 (NKJV) *And I will put enmity between you and the woman, and between your seed and her Seed; He shall bruise your head, and you shall bruise His heel.* This was the first mention of the plan of salvation and the seed of the woman is Christ, who will come to redeem mankind back to God. On the surface it seems it would have been less costly if our Creator allowed us to die right there and then in the Garden of Eden. From Satan's point of view, it should have been so, but his hope was shattered when the pronouncement of the woman's seed (Jesus) would give His life for all. The amazing grace of Christ would be brought low to save mankind! The law of God dictates that mankind should die in their sins, but it is indeed true that the grace of God abounds! *Moreover, the law entered that the offense might abound. But where sin abounded, grace abounded much more.* (Romans 5:20, NKJV).

Sin began in heaven, but the grace of God began there too. The whole universe was holding its breath to see the outcome of the first war. *And war broke out in heaven: Michael and his angels fought with the dragon; and the dragon and his angels fought, ⁸but they did not prevail, nor was a place found for them in heaven any longer. ⁹So the great dragon was cast out, that serpent of old, called the Devil and Satan, who deceives the whole world; he was cast to the earth, and his angels were cast out with him.* (Revelation 12:7-9, NKJV). And while the war continues on Earth, with humans becoming involved via Adam and Eve, God sent His Son to once and for all, put an end to sin and the war.

At the end of time, when Christ returns, he would have judged mankind for sin. *For the Father judges no one, but has committed all judgment to the Son.* (John 5:22, NKJV). So while grace abounds, let's take hold of Jesus and His amazing grace, while it's still available! With His grace we are more than conquerors.

William Layton Nelson, August 3, 2004.

DAY 22

Angry Billows

I was reading the news about Ivan, one of the world's deadliest hurricanes, which left in its wake a pathway of destruction. It also left its mark on Jamaica and made a mess of the only highway leading to the airport in Kingston. Twenty-five years ago, I would often sit on the shoulder of the highway and wondered if the raging waves on one side of the ocean would cross over onto the other side of the highway and disrupt the calm waters where the river kisses the sea. However, the retaining walls forming a bumper were no match for Ivan, even they gave in to its fury.

Angry Billows

The billows are angry at those rocks
Standing in their way, and so does the devil,
when we go to God in prayer.
My friend do not you worry about what
the devil will do to you; just put your trust in Jesus,
He'll carry you through the angry billows. He held the whole
world in the palm of His hands. He made every
thing good; they were pleasing to Him.
But only humankind, yes we made Him regret.

I know that I will never be wanting,
if I put my trust in my God. Lord you
walked on the water, and I believe you can
save me. So I will never worry about what
the devil will do.
I believe in Jesus, He will
carry me through all the storms of life and

be with me. He held the whole world in the
palm of His hands. He made everything good,
He said was pleased. But only Humankind,
we made Him regret.

You have said I am no more a servant,
but a friend, help me to give of my best to
you and to my fellowmen. You have done it
Lord so please help me with joyful heart,
to do likewise. Help me not to think or worry
about the sorrow, hardship or pain;
knowing that one day with you I shall ever
reign. You made everything good,
but only humankind, we made you regret.

Lord, today here I am standing on the
banks of life's sea, O stretch down thy
hand and take hold of me. Guide me
through the perils of life, O Lord,
please help Me. Through your grace
I shall live up to what you expect of me,
even if I have to suffer or die for
your Cause. You held the whole world,
in the palm of His Hands, You made
everything good, you were pleased.
But only humankind, made you regret.

Father, though angry billows should
beat at the foundation of my life,
cement me down firm on the rock of
your blessed Son, Jesus Christ. Then I
shall rest in peace, when I face the end
my life, and one day I shall cross over
the Jasper sea, to be with thee.
There in a world where no angry billows
will ever threaten or conquer me.

Where it will be our will, and our delight
to worship thee in love, for all eternity;
there in our homeland beyond the
angry billows.

Song *Angry Billows*. Lyrics & Music written by William Layton Nelson. Copyright © 1977.

William Layton Nelson, July 26, 1978.

DAY 23

Dangerous Detours

---

*Do you not know that those who run in a race all run, but one
receives the prize? Run in such a way that you may obtain it. ²⁵And
everyone who competes for the prize is temperate in all things. Now
they do it to obtain a perishable crown, but we for an imperishable
crown. ²⁶Therefore I run thus: not with uncertainty. Thus I fight:
not as one who beats the air. ²⁷But I discipline my body and bring
it into subjection, lest, when I have preached to others, I myself
should become disqualified.* (1 Corinthians 9:24-27, NKJV).

The Bible warns us about becoming distracted on our life's journey and on
being tempted to take dangerous detours.

Some time ago I dreamt I was traveling, and I came upon a beautiful
garden by the side of the road. To view the garden, you must get off the
straight path and take another pathway, off to the side. I love flowers, so
I took the garden path to admire the roses. I heard the waterfall in the
distance and followed the sound. I got as close as I could to the edge of a
ravine but couldn't see the waterfall. I was about to move a little closer to
the edge when I looked down at my feet. To my astonishing discovery, what
I thought to be green grass was indeed green carpet. The section nearest to
the edge was wet, and the precipitation formed a sheet of ice on it. I realized
that I was in grave danger because my feet were already planted on the ice.
Had it not been for someone else in the garden, who grabbed my arm and
pulled me to safety, I would have fallen over the precipice and die.

The Lord wants us to take note of His warnings, that while we are
traveling on life's highway, those detours we see, in most cases, they were
not constructed by the Lord but by the enemy who wants to distract us and
lure us away from the straight and narrow path. The vineyards, meadows,
and swinging gardens which we believe we must have in life, lead to a

popular path taken by many and they become lost in the sensation of the temptation. Our Savior warned against choosing the popular path over the more unpopular one.

Enter by the narrow gate; for wide is the gate and broad is the way that leads to destruction, and there are many who go in by it. [14]Because narrow is the gate and [b]difficult is the way which leads to life, and there are few who find it. (Matthew 7:13-14, NKJV).

The beautiful Garden of Eden is waiting for us at the end of the straight and narrow road. If you notice it did say straight, but it does not say smooth and flat! Sure you will find bumps along the way, which could cause difficulty in your life at times. That could well be the way God designed it for us. Sometimes it takes a rugged life to clean us up. He made it that way so that we can stay alert, because staying focused is altogether important to receiving the gift of eternal life.

I remember when growing up on the farm, at a certain time during the year we would run low on things like breadfruit, coconut, and avocado. But there is a place called Free Mountain, in St. James Jamaica, where you could find out-of-season food items in abundance! We had to walk along a narrow-rugged track, passing high rocks and going through a very short tunnel to reach the other side where the temperature drops and the cloudy mist lovingly caresses the gigantic trees, towering upward toward the sky. Some trees were even perching from atop the high rocky slopes; they were faithfully guarding the fruitful meadow. The sun had but a little chance to penetrate the tall, massive, clustered branches. The fruits were large and beautiful! Each time I read Matthew 7 which talks about narrow is the way, it always reminds me of this beautiful meadow. If we can only but endure the hardship we face in life, the narrow road we must walk will become more bearable.

I pray that whenever we are tempted to take detours and distract ourselves with these finer things of this present life, that the Holy Spirit will remind us that they will one day pass away. However, what is long lasting and forever are the gifts that God plans to give us at the end of the straight and narrow road. There is also a crown of life waiting for those who have remained faithful and steadfast in the race. Let's remember to run [the race] in such a way that [we] may obtain it. (1 Corinthians 9:24b, NKJV).

William Layton Nelson, July 26, 2004.

DAY 24

Heavenly Love

---

*For God so loved the world that He gave His only begotten
Son, that whoever believes in Him should not perish
but have everlasting life.* (John 3: 16, NKJV).

We have been given the opportunity to live good lives as we have access
to Christ who redeems us to God, and to the Comforter who draw us to
the Redeemer. *The Lord has appeared of old to me, saying: Yes, I have loved
you with an everlasting love; Therefore with lovingkindness I have drawn you.*
(Jeremiah 31: 3, NKJV).

This is great news! It is quite natural that the Lord God loves us
because He made us and wants to bestow on us His Heavenly love. He is
a Father who cares for His children, and we especially see and experience
this in situations of His Divine intervention. It is during these times that
He makes exceptions and dispatches angels, moving faster than the speed
of light to come to our aid. Let me give you an idea of how that works. We
must remember also that we were made in His image and that caring spirit
is somewhere within all of us as well. Imagine walking with your little
child along the sidewalk on the Main Street in your City. Let's say your
child pulls away from your grasp, and before you can get a grip of what is
happening your child suddenly cries out for help! At that very moment you
look up and a car or a vicious dog is bearing down on that child.

What would you do?

How would you react? Faster than lightening, I would say.

Our first inclination is to save the child at all costs. That is our nature,
it is a built-in sensor. God made us that way. Just as we would want to
save the child, there are instances when God intervenes to save us from the
devil's schemes. God wants us to remember always that He is our refuge
and strength. The evil one is on a mission and that is to destroy God's

people, but we must not allow that to deter us because we have the hand of the mighty God under us. *The eternal God is your refuge, and underneath are the everlasting arms; He will thrust out the enemy from before you, And will say, ˜Destroy!* (Deuteronomy 33: 27, NKJV).

God bridges the gap between heaven's time and our time. I must point out that whatsoever crises we face, our heavenly Father and Jesus Christ can take care of them for us. Rely wholly on the power and wisdom of the Almighty if you are not doing so already. I pray that this coming week, you will start walking down that path in which trusting in God becomes routine. Let's face it, we need the Lord every passing hour, don't we?

William Layton Nelson, August 11, 2004

DAY 25

What Color is Jesus' Love

*Greater love hath no man than this, that a man lay
down his life for his friends.* *14 Ye are my friends, if ye do
whatsoever I command you.* (John 15:13-14, NKJV).

Jesus divulged a prophetic word of the kind of love he possessed for his
disciples and friends in the weeks leading up to his death.

He declared His love for his friends in such a statement: *Greater love
hath no man than this, that a man lay down his life for his friends.* (John
15:13, NKJV).

As He is our brother and our friend, we can say Jesus expressed his
love for the world!

When He came to Earth, there were people of different cultures,
ethnicities, and colors; yet He came. He embraced all. His love is not
divided into sections, nationalities, and colors. It's not according to party
affiliation and the color of money.

His love is therefore non-discriminatory.

His love has no color.

If then He is our brother and friend, then all who live are also our
brothers and friends. Let us show all men the same love that Jesus shows
us; a love devoid of color and discrimination.

Discrimination is presumptuous. It means that as humans we disregard
God's creative diversity. As there are many kinds of animals and trees, each
after their own kind (diverse species), so are humans created in diversity
and beauty. Discrimination also disregards God's pronunciation of His
creation as good!

The Bible tells us that we are *fearfully and wonderfully made* and
the Psalmist continued to say, *Marvelous are [His] works!* (Psalm 139:14,
NKJV). But humans are not satisfied with the way God made them, so

they dismiss the work of the Creator and instead create dark barriers of rudeness and indifference against people of other race or color.

Let's remember today that the center of our universe is Christ who called His creation good. Who are we to say otherwise?

Pray that God will unite our hearts with His love which is devoid of hate and discrimination. Instead, ask that His perfect love will fill our hearts.

William Layton Nelson, April 24, 2002.

DAY 26

Our Missionary Work at Home

During the night Paul had a vision of a man of Macedonia standing and begging him, "Come over to Macedonia and help us.¹⁰ After Paul had seen the vision, we got ready at once to leave for Macedonia, concluding that God had called us to preach the gospel to them. (Acts 16:9-10, NKJV).

For years we have been reading and hearing about the call to Macedonia. The Macedonian call is a legitimate call to respond to Christ's command: *Go therefore and make disciples of all the nations, baptizing them in the name of the Father and of the Son and of the Holy Spirit.* (Matthew 28:19, NKJV). Paul, on his second missionary journey, responded to the call after receiving a vision to preach the gospel in Macedonia:

During the night Paul had a vision of a man of Macedonia standing and begging him, "Come over to Macedonia and help us. ¹⁰ After Paul had seen the vision, we got ready at once to leave for Macedonia, concluding that God had called us to preach the gospel to them. (Acts 16:9-10, NKJV).

Today, Christians refer to the phrase Macedonian call when talking about going to foreign countries to preach the message of Christ. This is in response to the Christ's instructions about the gospel and the end times. *And this gospel of the kingdom will be preached in all the world as a witness to all the nations, and then the end will come.* (Matthew 24: 14, NKJV).

However, the Macedonian call can also refer to domestic mission. While we are intent on looking out and over the fence, eagerly striving to reach those who are on the other side, let us remember those closest to us at home who are also in need of salvation.

In a baseball game, we begin at the home plate, hit the ball, run around the bases and it's important to get back to the home plate. So it is with the gospel; we tend to overlook the importance of starting out at home, thereby leaving behind unfinished work with those closest to us. From personal experience, I have seen first-hand the need to reach family members with the gospel. There have been instances where family members bemoan the passing of loved ones who never had the chance to accept Christ as their Savior.

Let me stress that it is important for us to live a balanced life, as human beings and as children of God. Therefore, let us not revert to saying:

I am looking out for me and myself alone.

If we neglect to heed the call to go and we are spending too much time concentrating on self, then we are satisfying our own selfish motives. So, let's begin with those closest to us. Begin at the home plate.

William Layton Nelson, July 22, 2004.

DAY 27

My Life as a Prisoner

So he answered and said to me: This is the word of the Lord
to Zerubbabel: Not by might nor by power, but by My Spirit,
Says the Lord of hosts. (Zechariah 4:6, NKJV).

All of us have been prisoners at one time or another so please sit upright in your seats as I attempt to take you back in time, when I was a prisoner to popularity. Those days I spent behind those walls were wasted years. My heart was engulfed with the desire to be a part of the popular crowd. Even from the days of my childhood, I strive to befriend people who were somebody! Right!

Due to the low value I placed on my own importance, deceived by society, my eyes were only able to see the importance of my existence through such narrow margins. I truly believe that to live such a life is a terrible way to occupy one's borrowed time in this world. You hate being who you are, not that you are a bad person but just because you are not popular. When you are in that type of prison, you tend to turn your back on people who can't offer you momentary popularity.

Those you ignored, oftentimes in later years, are the ones who are being sought after. They slowly built their lives on solid foundations with character traits that are admirable.

For many years I found that my life as a prisoner to popularity, yielded me no dividends. These days I do reach out to others but for a different reason; that is, to draw them to the character of Jesus Christ, who has the only popularity that really matters! To be popular in doing the things of the Savior; to be filled with the Holy Ghost, where others can see His light shining in and through you, is the desire which should engulf our hearts. I must warn you that we must guard against adoring our brothers and sisters in our churches. I know we mean them well but not everyone can handle a flurry of praise. For those who are extra talented, whenever people praise you, just forward the praise to the Holy Spirit, Jesus and our heavenly Father. Remember, it's not by [your] might nor by [your] power, but by My Spirit, says the Lord of hosts. (Zechariah 4:6, NKJV).

I believe the sooner we realize we cannot do anything without His power, the sooner our lives will be enriched. The empowerment one feels knowing that all things are possible with an all-powerful God who is on your side, is liberating. The apostle Paul who himself was set free from his overzealous mission of doom, was reconciled to a more empowered life. *Casting down arguments and every high thing that exalts itself against the knowledge of God, bringing every thought into captivity to the obedience of Christ.* (2 Corinthians 10:5, NKJV).

He also set the thief on the cross free, who received salvation that day. Nothing he did by his might or power, but eternal grace was extended by the all-saving power of Christ.

He Saved Me

1. My soul was lost; I saw no hope in sight,
I looked to Jesus; He knew just what to do
for me. He lifted me up, and held me close
to Him, and with gentle words He whispered:
I'll save you.

Refrain: He saved me; yes, He saved me.
He gently wiped my guilt and shame away.
He saved me; yes, He saved me.
From the valley of despair, He saved me.

2. If your soul feels lost and in despair today,
look to Jesus, He'll know just what to do for you.
He will lift you up, and hold you oh so close
to His breast. With gentle words He'll whisper,
I'll help you.

Song *He Saved Me,* Inspirational. Lyrics & Music by William Layton Nelson, ©2004.

Yes, Jesus saving power is far reaching; even to the end of time so unite with Him now.

William Layton Nelson, September 19, 2004.

DAY 28

Our Manna

---

*So when the children of Israel saw it, they said to one another, ˜What
is it? For they did not know what it was. And Moses said to them,
This is the bread which the Lord has given you
to eat.* (Exodus 16:15, NKJV).

All scriptures are fascinating in my opinion to say the least! Each part of
the written word of God is an important lesson for us. It was important
for those who lived back then, and it still applies to us today. One major
point that stands out in the stories of the Bible, especially within the Old
Testament, is dissatisfaction of God's people.

It was 3am and I was awake, thinking about my experience that week,
how the Lord blessed me by providing manna. The manna He provided
wasn't food on a plate, instead I was grateful for the gift we oftentimes
overlook, God's love. It is so easy to forget that He uses many channels of
blessings to place value in our lives.

According to Webster's dictionary, one definition of manna is:
Anything of value that one receives unexpectedly.

That week I had received a pocketful of manna. No, it wasn't cash, but
a kindly appreciated deed from someone I met for the first time. I have had
many of those in my lifetime, how about you?

Ever since creation, God has always provided for His children. He
provides for all. *He makes His sun rise on the evil and on the good, and sends
rain on the just and on the unjust.* (Matthew 5:45, NKJV). I am so grateful
God is not like men; with His power, no telling what some of us would
have done to folks who might have done us wrong!

God provides for us and blesses us in many ways, and we should always
give thanks, no matter what! If you were not doing so before, I pray that
you will start looking out for the manna He has so bountifully provided

for you, your family, and your friends. You know as well as I do that it's not easy sometimes, but we should be glad when our friends and our neighbors prosper. Do you know what I think? I think that if you pause to look over the blessings you have received, starting this week, I am sure next week you will still be tallying up His goodness. God keeps on blessing, doesn't He?

May I remind you that you should not forget to thank Him for the blessings coming your way!

William Layton Nelson, September 17, 2004.

DAY 29

Preparedness

For as in the days before the flood, they were eating and drinking,
marrying and giving in marriage, until the day that Noah entered the
ark, ^{39} and did not know until the flood came and took them all away,
so also will the coming of the Son of Man be. Matthew 24:38-39.

Preparedness is the key to being ready for Christ and His coming kingdom. Are you prepared for that event? Are you ready for Jesus to come? Are you doing everything possible to let your friends and your neighbors be aware of this?

Like the changes in the weather to indicate a coming storm or hurricane, so too should we be aware of the warning signs of Jesus' soon return. The saying the great day is coming, is just as relevant today as it was in the time of the disciples. The signs are showing it is near. In Revelation 6:17 (NKJV) John spoke of that day, *For the great day of His wrath has come, and who is able to stand?*

Who will be able to stand? Who is prepared for such a glorious return, and can we stand before His majestic splendor?

Stop and ask yourself the question because it's a sobering one. Joel, the prophet, asked *who can endure it?*

The Lord gives voice before His army, For His camp is very great; For strong is the One who executes His word. For the day of the Lord is great and very terrible; Who can endure it? (Joel 2:11, NKJV).

Joel wondered if mankind was prepared to face a righteous God.

Hundreds of thousands of people prepare ahead of time before a hurricane strikes their homes; even while it's hundreds of miles out on the ocean. But many fail to prepare for eternity, thinking they have plenty of time. However, this is a deceit of the devil.

We tell ourselves:

I have plenty of time, so it's all right to give my heart to Christ when I get older.

I have plenty of time, so it is okay to start living right, later.

But Jesus warns us that the people of Noah's time had the same thoughts. They had forgotten about God and were unrighteous and carried on with life as usual although Noah preached for 120 years. Noah warned of the impending doom, but only Noah and his family were preparing to enter the ark. When the flood waters came, they died because they were not obedient as Noah was.

For as in the days before the flood, they were eating and drinking, marrying and giving in marriage, until the day that Noah entered the ark, And did not know until the flood came and took them all away, so also will the coming of the Son of Man be. (Matthew 24:38-39, NKJV).

In Luke 12:40 (NKJV) our Savior warns: *Therefore you also be ready, for the Son of Man is coming at an hour you do not expect.*

I am prayerfully wishing we are all ready.

William Layton Nelson, September 22, 2004.

DAY 30

The Awakening Cry!

For this is he who was spoken of by the prophet Isaiah, saying:
The voice of one crying in the wilderness: ʹPrepare the way of the
Lord; Make His paths straight. (Matthew 3:3, NKJV)

There is an awakening cry, or an alarm sounded for the coming of the Savior. However, are we too busy or distracted to hear the alarm? The cry is for us to ʹtrim our lamps because we are *the light of the world.* Matthew 5:14 (NKJV). We have what people need, the gospel; are we making it available to them?

Prepare the way of the Lord suggests preparation for His arrival. How prepared are we to meet Him, and are we helping others to prepare too? The question is this, how can we prepare the way of the Lord? First, we must know who we are. Be always hungry to feast on His word. We need to have our minds filled with a desire of soul winning and be eager to see people come to the knowledge of the sweetness of God's love. Only then, will we be ready to do as He commands. *And He said to them, ʹGo into all the world and preach the gospel to every creature.* (Mark 16:15, NKJV).

The fields are ripe, waiting to be harvested, are you ready and willing to lend your voice, your hands, your feet, and your time to the Holy Spirit? Are you up to it? Are you eager to be that voice that sounds the alarm?

We must get out to where those in need are and invite them into the marriage supper of the Lamb! Fortify ourselves with the Word and the Holy Spirit, and without reservation and with a praying attitude, let's share the good news of the gospel.

The echoing of the awakening cry should be heard more often in these last days.

William Layton Nelson, July 14, 2004.

DAY 31

The Brighter Side of Life

---

*For I know the thoughts that I think toward you, says
the Lord, thoughts of peace and not of evil, to give you a
future and a hope.* (Jeremiah 29:11, NKJV).

Life sometimes can be like a waterwheel. It comes to the surface to dispose of its content then goes back down once more. The portion of the wheel which is coming out from the water is filled with sparkling hope for those waiting to have it emptied into their buckets. Gradually those buckets, which brought the water up, empty their contents before dipping again into the flowing stream. Our lives are like that sometimes, bountiful and abundant, and yet dry and in need at other times. Having God in our lives and sincere friends, bring hope when all goes dim. Hope is looking at the brighter side of life. It's a gift of God that doesn't disappoint.

Now hope does not disappoint, because the love of God has been poured out in our hearts by the Holy Spirit who was given to us. (Romans 5:5, NKJV).

Trusting in the One in whom all things are possible, is the beginning of a walk of faith in a God who is more than able to open the firmament of heaven and pour out to us His blessings. The blessings may not come in the way we envision them. However, He always keeps His promises, and He knows best.

King David must have watched the people pulling up the water from his wells to water his vineyards. He must have watched the birds as they wake up early in the morning hoping to find food. He knew that his heavenly Father was the one who made all things possible. He was not a poor man; he had wealth, yet he declared:

My soul, wait silently for God alone, For my expectation is from Him. (Psalms 62: 5, NKJV).

The best kind of waiting is to wait expectantly or to wait in hope.

This means, you've approached the Savior with your request and now you expectantly wait. The Lord is not slack concerning his promise[s] (2 Peter 3:9), NKJV). His intentions for us are pure, to give us a hope:

For I know the thoughts that I think toward you, says the Lord, thoughts of peace and not of evil, to give you a future and a hope. (Jeremiah 29:11, NKJV).

God bless you, dear Christian friends.

William Layton Nelson, June 6, 2003.

DAY 32

Nothing but the best!

Recently in the parking lot of our church, I bid the pastor goodbye, and I continued by saying:

Say hi to the family!

He stopped with a puzzled look on his face. He said:

To say hi, does not sound right, you always say "give my love to the family. That sounds better! Nothing but the best!

It was early Sabbath afternoon, everyone was tired from the long week of participating in the Vacation Bible School project, especially the pastor, who commuted two and a half hours one way most of the evenings to get there. He could have allowed it to slip by, but now he would not accept anything less than the best, to take to his beloved family. Well, I do not think that anyone in their right mind would think of blaming him for the stance he had taken.

Later that afternoon, as I tried to unwind from the event of the whole week, I thought about the look on the pastor's face and his proclamation. I also thought about our heavenly Father. When mankind turned away from Him in the Garden of Eden, He was disappointed. He felt rejected, yet He gave His best to us in the gift of His Son Jesus. Nothing but the best! As the blood flowed from Christ's sinless body and mingled with the dust when He walked toward the hill of death, He was fulfilling the Father's will by giving the best of Himself to redeem His creation. Nothing but the best! Nothing but the Blood of Jesus which gives us eternal life!

This week as you pause to look back at maybe just a few days or you could even go as far back as you want to venture, take the time to ask yourself:

Did I genuinely give of my best to others? Did I shortchange someone by withholding my affections? It could be your wife, your husband, your children, your parents, or your friends.

During those hours, days or weeks, did you give of your best to the Master? Our heavenly Father did. It is so stated in His written word. *For God so loved the world that He gave His only begotten Son, that whoever believes in Him should not perish but have everlasting life.* (John 3: 16, NKJV).

That wonderful story is also written in a song:

For God so loved the world that He gave His only Son,
to die on Calvary's tree, from sin to set me free.
One day He's coming back, what a glory that will be,
wonderful His love to me. Pelangi Kasih by Nikita " Praise & Worship, ©2012.

For the child of God, and for the most wretched sinner, those words should come as a comfort and instill hope in our hearts. This should bring peace to any troubled soul. We should not hesitate to accept God's love, and then impart it to our friends and the world.

William Layton Nelson, June 19, 2004.

DAY 33

Does God Protect the Foolish?

For we ourselves were also once foolish, disobedient, deceived, serving various lusts and pleasures, living in malice and envy, hateful and hating one another. ⁴But when the kindness and the love of God our Savior toward man appeared, ⁵not by works of righteousness which we have done, but according to His mercy He saved us, through the washing of regeneration and renewing of the Holy Spirit. (Titus 3:3-5, NKJV).

In the book of Titus, Paul had an extraordinary experience on the road to Damascus. In his letter to Titus, Paul alluded to his once foolish decision to persecute the Christians. However, in the same letter, he spoke about God's grace and forgiveness and newness in Christ:

For we ourselves were also once foolish, disobedient, deceived, serving various lusts and pleasures, living in malice and envy, hateful and hating one another. ⁴But when the kindness and the love of God our Savior toward man appeared, ⁵not by works of righteousness which we have done, but according to His mercy He saved us, through the washing of regeneration and renewing of the Holy Spirit. (Titus 3:3-5, NKJV).

While Paul speaks of a literal place (on the road to Damascus), let's reflect on the many roads on which we've traveled (figuratively), that were forbidden, dangerous and foolish.

I have traveled many of those roads, how about you?

Unlike Paul, I knew but I did nevertheless! How about you?

I was acting foolishly and with a stubborn attitude. I was defying the admonition of God and crossing boundaries to selfishly obtain gratification. Several times I could have lost my life, but God commanded His angels to watch over me. How about you?

The gift of His only Son is a perfect example of how He protects the foolish.

But God demonstrates His own love toward us, in that while we were still sinners, Christ died for us. (Romans 5:8, NKJV).

Another example can be found in the book of Jonah, which speaks about Jonah's disobedience to God's commands. Jonah foolishly believed he knew the people of Nineveh much better than God and thought they didn't deserve God's grace. Foolishly, he tried to hide from God by going the opposite direction, down into the bottom of a ship heading for Tarshish.

But can we hide from God?

Instead of the belly of a ship, the Lord prepared the belly of a large fish for Jonah, and his experience was not a pleasant one. God heard his call from the ocean's depth, and He saved him.

Was it an accident that the fish was just waiting there? Of course not!

Let us read a verse in the Bible and see what conclusion we can come to. *Now the Lord had prepared a great fish to swallow Jonah. And Jonah was in the belly of the fish three days and three nights.* (Jonah 1:17, NKJV).

Here is the conclusion of the whole matter - God is patient with our foolishness, and while he doesn't save us from it, He offers His protection and uses it as a teaching moment (as He did with Jonah and Paul) for us to better understand Him.

Our God is a loving and merciful God. Let me note that He is the same God who commanded His angels to watch over Moses, Job, Queen Ester, Joseph, Daniel in the lion's den, Jonah, the three Hebrew boys, Paul; we could go on and on. God never changes.

For I am the Lord, I do not change; Therefore you are not consumed, O sons of Jacob. (Malachi 3:6, NKJV).

It does not matter how stupid and inadequate we feel because we have acted foolishly, God will pardon and forgive. Jeremiah said: *The voice of joy and the voice of gladness, the voice of the bridegroom and the voice of the bride, the voice of those who will say: ¯Praise the Lord of hosts, For the Lord is good, For His mercy endures forever and of those who will bring the sacrifice of praise into the house of the Lord. For I will cause the captives of the land to return as at the first, says the Lord.* (Jeremiah 33:11, NKJV).

God's aim is to save humankind from destruction. He is longsuffering (patient) toward us (2 Peter 3:9, NKJV) *The Lord is not slack concerning His promise, as some count slackness, but is longsuffering toward us, not willing that any should perish but that all should come to repentance.*

Let's however strive to keep within the boundaries of His grace and not push beyond our limit as we are reminded:

Behold, I am coming quickly, and My reward is with Me, to give to every one according to his work. (Revelation 22:12, NKJV).

May God bless you.

William Layton Nelson, June 1, 2004.

DAY 34

Youth, the Future Church?

A common misunderstanding in our churches today stems from the following statement:

Our youth are the future church.

However, for the most part, they are wrong!

It is a misconception. The youth are here today, are they not?

They are now, not only for tomorrow, *but now!*

I don't think that Jesus consulted the disciples, whether He should see the children who came to Him. He told them bluntly, that they should allow the parents to bring their children to Him!

But Jesus said, "Let the little children come to Me, and do not forbid them; for of such is the kingdom of heaven. (Matthew 19:14, NKJV).

Jesus is our big brother; therefore, He has the right to call all of us children. Children are an integral part of the church. While they are tomorrow's congregation, they are also today's leaders, missionaries, and workers! Trained in the way of Christ, children can bring their peers to Christ. Why do we need to prepare them only for tomorrow, when they can begin the work of Christ today?

The youth have been offered a lot by Jesus. They have been gifted with talents that are useful in the ministry of Christ, and older members of the congregation should be encouraging and supportive, as was Eli in the case of Samuel.

There may be some things the youth might not fully understand, as did Samuel in his life while He lived with Eli. However, adults should be happy to help in whatever way they can. Samuel was only a lad, when the Lord called him to be His witness. I am hoping you can find the time to read in the book of Samuel for yourselves where he obeyed Eli's counsel and surrendered his will to the Lord. *Therefore Eli said to Samuel, Go, lie down; and it shall be, if He calls you, that you must say, "Speak, Lord, for*

Your servant hears. So Samuel went and lay down in his place. (1 Samuel 3:9, NKJV).

Some may find it difficult in believing this, but just like Samuel, God is calling young people for His purpose. Therefore, let us all work together; let us do what we can for our Savior. Whatever talents God has loaned you, use it in His service. Look all around you and find someone in need; help someone today, even though it may be a small neighborly deed.

Council to the youth: Remember to show respect to the elderly because in them can be found a wealth of knowledge and wisdom. And while you may be groomed today to be tomorrow's General Conference President, always remember the church is now! You are needed now, so step up and fill those empty places! Are you willing to let God use you as a channel through which He can bless others?

William Layton Nelson, April 11, 2004.

DAY 35

Crushed Dreams

When your dreams are crushed, do you feel bitter about some of the choices you have made in your life? The future stands as an insurmountable mountain and your path in life seems fraught with obstacles, and you don't know what to do next. I am afraid I cannot tell you your next move, but I can tell you that we've all had crushed dreams that have left us feeling bitter and disappointed and unsure about the future. I can also tell you that everything is going to be alright.

You know when we find ourselves in that situation; way out in leftfield, without any meaningful friend, someone on whom you can lean on, we need to get closer to Christ, the Lighthouse who illuminates our path.

Several years ago, I had a project near and dear to my heart that ended in disappointment. I had stretched my limited resources extremely thin, with the hope that soon the strain would ease, and I would start reaping from the field of sacrificial endeavors. To my dismay and disappointment, my dreams were suddenly crushed, and all expectations died with it!

It's at these times, we tend to ask ourselves:

What's next? I thought this was it, but now what do I do?

Or, do I start again?

It's also at these times when we hold God's promises close to our hearts and try to recall what he says about our future. One beautiful promise that He has given to us is found in the book of Jeremiah. The people of Israel were afraid and unsure about their future because they were taken into captivity to Babylon. Jeremiah, the prophet of God, wrote a letter to the remainder of the elders who were also taken from Jerusalem to Babylon. The letter (found in Jeremiah 29: 4-32) delivered the message of God's promise of hope and a future; it was written to uplift the spirits of the people and to ease the bitterness they felt about their crushed dreams. Near the beginning of the letter, God made a promise that He has a beautiful future prepared for them!

For I know the thoughts that I think toward you, says the Lord, thoughts of peace and not of evil, to give you a future and a hope. (Jeremiah 29:11, NKJV).

Never despair. It's said, when one door closes, another opens and what God closes, no man open; and what He opens, no one can shut. Therefore, if today your dreams are crushed, then lean on His promise that He has better in store for you!

William Layton Nelson, August 8, 2004.

DAY 36

Empty Fruit Basket

You are the salt of the earth; but if the salt loses its flavor, how shall it be seasoned? It is then good for nothing but to be thrown out and trampled underfoot by men. (Mathew 5:13, NKJV).

I am pretty sure that no one wants to or plans to become asphalt (the stuff our roadways are made of) to be trampled or driven over, but that is exactly what Jesus said would become of people who are useless. Sounds a little harsh, doesn't it?

I understood the verse in Matthew as I sat at the dinner table looking at the empty fruit basket sitting in the center of it. It suddenly seemed offensive.

Why was it there? It was like an empty container taking up space!

I reached forward to remove it, but hesitated. Even though it was carefully woven with a special straw and beautiful to look at, currently it served no purpose and should be put away on the kitchen counter until we bought more fruits!

However, I left the basket on the table, rationalizing that the only reason it served no purpose at the time is, it's waiting to be filled. It's an empty vessel waiting to be filled! Aren't we all?

Jesus illustrated to his disciples the uselessness of stunted Christianity through his unusual interaction with the fig tree.

And seeing a fig tree by the road, He came to it and found nothing on it but leaves, and said to it, Let no fruit grow on you ever again. Immediately the fig tree withered away. (Matthew 21:19, NKJV).

Notice the fig tree suddenly became firewood but let us also read Luke 13: 6-9 about the story of another fig tree.

He also spoke this parable: A certain man had a fig tree planted in his vineyard, and he came seeking fruit on it and found none. ⁷Then he said to the keeper of his vineyard, ˜Look, for three years I have come seeking fruit on this fig tree and find none. Cut it down; why does it use up the ground?⁸But he answered and said to him, Sir, let it alone this year also, until I dig around it and fertilize it. ⁹And if it bears fruit, well. But if not, after that you can cut it down. (Luke 13: 6-9, NKJV).

Jesus knew that the fig tree which withered away and became firewood would never bear fruit. However, the fig tree in the book of Luke had the potential to bear fruit, like the basket which would be worthwhile once it's filled with fruit.

Could it be possible that the fig trees in both parables represented people? And is it also possible that the dresser of the vineyard is Christ? Some may argue that it is the Holy Spirit, while others have different interpretations altogether.

My experience with the empty fruit basket highlights both parts of the parables wanting to put it away but also wanting to show some mercy. It is also a possibility that Jesus (the keeper of the vineyard) was watching both fig trees for some time.

In such a case, He knows best the outcome of each fig tree, and as a result, one was cursed into damnation and grace and mercy was extended to the other. We are empty vessels waiting to be filled by the Holy Spirit if we would let Him. However, we become useless when as Christians we bear no fruit; that is, we are empty with nothing to give.

Here are the questions we need to ask ourselves:

Am I like any of the fig trees?

And if so, which one?

How long has it been since I have not borne any fruit for the Master?

Am I like the empty fruit basket, sitting on the table with nothing to give?

Am I sitting pretty within the church pews, or am I ripe with the fruits of the Spirit of love, joy, peace, long-suffering, gentleness, goodness, faith, meekness, and temperance?

Will others be able see Jesus in me?

William Layton Nelson, September 22, 2004.

DAY 37

Why Does God Permit Suffering?

Therefore, just as through one man sin entered the world,
and death through sin, and thus death spread to all men,
because all sinned. (Romans 5:12, NKJV).

My friend, I believe that all of us know what the word sin means? Romans 5:12 reads:

Therefore, just as through one man sin entered the world, and death through sin, and thus death spread to all men, because all sinned. (Romans 5:12, NKJV).

Sin entered the world through Adam, and so did the consequence of sin which is death. *For the wages of sin is death, but the gift of God is eternal life in Christ Jesus our Lord.* (Romans 6:23, NKJV).

If God had destroyed sin at the very beginning when Adam and Eve disobeyed, then they would have died right away. But wouldn't that have left doubts with the whole universe concerning His treatment of His subjects. He would be accused of being harsh and merciless.

Before sin, there was no death; no tears; no sadness and no suffering. These negative effects of sin become a part of our everyday life during the generations. Man's encounter with sin is daily and the consequences are ongoing.

The Bible has many instances of God's warning against sin.

And [He] said, If you diligently heed the voice of the Lord your God and do what is right in His sight, give ear to His commandments and keep all His statutes, I will put none of the diseases on you which I have brought on the Egyptians. For I am the Lord who heals you. Exodus 15:26, NKJV).

If My people who are called by My name will humble themselves, and pray and seek My face, and turn from their wicked ways, then I will hear from heaven, and will forgive their sin and heal their land. (2 Chronicles 7:14, NKJV).

As a result, sin and suffering will always be a part of our lives, until it is fully done away with at the return of Christ. But in the meantime, Christ, who is the resolution to sin, has gone to prepare a place for us where there will be no more death, sin nor suffering.

And I heard a loud voice from heaven saying, Behold, the tabernacle of God is with men, and He will dwell with them, and they shall be His people. God Himself will be with them and be their God. 4 And God will wipe away every tear from their eyes; there shall be no more death, nor sorrow, nor crying. There shall be no more pain, for the former things have passed away. (Revelation 21:3-4, NKJV).

I can only speak for myself, but from where I am sitting, and from what I see taking place in our world, makes me have a longing feeling for this place that John speaks about in Revelation 21. I pray that you are feeling the same way also, longing for home, where suffering will be history!

William Layton Nelson, September 19, 2004.

DAY 38

To Love Like God

The Lord has appeared of old to me, saying: Yes, I have loved
you with an everlasting love; Therefore with lovingkindness
I have drawn you. (Jeremiah 31:3, NKJV).

Agape love is known as the universal form of love because everyone experiences it, and it is not selfish and can be given freely. Humans are quite capable of agape love and we use it in many circumstances when we love our family, friends and even strangers. Agape love is demonstrated in several forms, such as support, joy for someone, and empathy.

The problem with agape love, however, is that while it's an active form of love, it can be conditional too. This happens when self gets in the way and out motives become selfish. Therefore, to love others the way the Father loves us, we must set our minds on Jesus so that His thoughts of love will transmit through to ours.

You will keep him in perfect peace, whose mind is stayed on You, because he trusts in You. (Isaiah 26:3, NKJV).

He declared to us that His love is an everlasting love. *The Lord has appeared of old to me, saying: ˉYes, I have loved you with an everlasting love; Therefore with lovingkindness I have drawn you.* (Jeremiah 31:3, NKJV).

God's love is unconditional. It's given freely to all mankind, despite our race, gender, and nationality. He loves us whether we accept Him or not. The disciples and the people Jesus met during His years on Earth, received His love freely. Lepers who were outcasts were treated with respect and compassion.

And it happened when He was in a certain city, that behold, a man who was full of leprosy saw Jesus; and he fell on his face and implored Him, saying, Lord, if You are willing, You can make me clean. ¹³Then He put out His hand

and touched him, saying, I am willing; be cleansed. Immediately the leprosy left him. (Luke 5:12-13, NKJV).

Notice Jesus touched the leper. There was no discrimination on the part of Jesus. Instead, His love for the leper as a child of God, shines through his action of healing.

Another example is found in Luke 8:43-48 (NKJV):

Now a woman, having a flow of blood for twelve years, who had spent all her livelihood on physicians and could not be healed by any, ⁴⁴came from behind and touched the border of His garment. And immediately her flow of blood stopped.

⁴⁵And Jesus said, Who touched Me?

When all denied it, Peter and those with him said, Master, the multitudes throng and press You, and You say, Who touched Me?

⁴⁶But Jesus said, Somebody touched Me, for I perceived power going out from Me.

Notice again that Jesus showed compassion to someone who is considered a sinner worthy of death. However, Jesus provided the one thing the Jewish leaders refused to give her, which is forgiveness, an attribute of agape love.

Jesus knows our sorrows, and He is acquainted with [our] grief. The grateful woman stepped forward to clear the matter up. (Luke 8:47-48, NKJV):

Now when the woman saw that she was not hidden, she came trembling; and falling down before Him, she declared to Him in the presence of all the people the reason she had touched Him and how she was healed immediately.

⁴⁸And He said to her, Daughter, be of good cheer; your faith has made you well. Go in peace.

Christs love in unconditional. Leave your burdens at His feet and allow the Holy Spirit to illuminate you with the light of glory, to go and do likewise; that is, love as He does!

William Layton Nelson, August 13, 2004.

DAY 39

Be Ye Also Ready!

Therefore you also be ready, for the Son of Man is coming at an hour you do not expect. (Matthew 24:44, NKJV).

Everyday people die. It happens so often that some have become calloused to it and consider it a natural part of life. But it was never God's intention for mankind to die. However, sin changed the dynamic of our eternal existence and as a result, death has become as natural as breathing.

While it may be so, we must, however, take precaution to prepare for it. Jesus cautions us to prepare for His second coming while we are alive:

Therefore you also be ready, for the Son of Man is coming at an hour you do not expect. (Matthew 24:44, NKJV).

There's reason for this; that is, there's no preparation in the grave. For those who have died before His return, the next time they regain consciousness is at the sound of the trumpet.

For the Lord Himself will descend from heaven with a shout, with the voice of an archangel, and with the trumpet of God. And the dead in Christ will rise first. (1 Thessalonians 4:16, NKJV).

Therefore, if they were not ready before they died, then it would have been too late. Participation in the first resurrection therefore means gaining eternal life.

Whether we die before Christ's return or we are alive to see the event, let's be diligent in our preparation to meet the Savior.

Even Solomon, in his time, observed the way people were laid back! He noticed the behavior of those around him who displayed a nonchalant attitude toward eternal life. He explained it this way.

Because the sentence against an evil work is not executed speedily, therefore the heart of the sons of men is fully set in them to do evil. (Ecclesiastes 8:11, NKJV).

Complacency in regard to our eternal life is the opposite of being ready. *Let us therefore [go] boldly to the throne of grace, that we may obtain mercy and find grace to help in time of need.* (Hebrews 4:16, NKJV). Our heavenly Father always provides a way for us to get out of darkness.

Let's accept His offer of grace.

William Layton Nelson, June 28, 2004.

DAY 40

Sanctified Vessels

But the Lord said to him, Go, for he is a chosen vessel of Mine to bear My name before Gentiles, kings, and the children of Israel. (Acts 9:15, NKJV).

As I look around me, I see vessels, people of God, faithfully taking on the challenge placed before them by the Son of God, the living Word (Jesus Christ) to *Go therefore and make disciples of all nations¦*.(Matthew 28:19a, NKJV).

Even before Paul's time, God relied on faithful witnesses to speak the word to a dying world. These have been sanctified vessels, to do the will of God and carry out His mission for mankind. To Ananias in Acts 9:15, Christ referred to Paul as His chosen vessel:

But the Lord said to him, Go, for he is a chosen vessel of Mine to bear My name before Gentiles, kings, and the children of Israel. (Acts 9:15, NKJV).

I am so glad that today we are also given the opportunity to be witnesses for Him. The mere fact that we are chosen vessels, we should be eager to proclaim ourselves God's true representatives. As Christ ministered to the early churches, so He will for the remnant church at the end of the age. But Paul advised that we should consider ourselves stewards of God's will, ready to be vessels of honor as we are filled with the Holy Spirit.

But in a great house there are not only vessels of gold and silver, but also of wood and clay, some for honor and some for dishonor. ²¹Therefore if anyone cleanses himself from the latter, he will be a vessel for honor, sanctified and useful for the Master, prepared for every good work. (2 Timothy 2: 20-21, NKJV).

True, we do a lot of good things in the church and for our fellow believers. However, what should be the true motive and attitude of a sanctified vessel? Many Christians are lacking the enthusiasm needed to successfully perform the task of the Great Commission. When we love Christ, we'll love as He does, wanting others to express His love, forgiveness, and grace. Not until we have the truth of God embedded in our hearts and minds, will we be able to have that unconditional love for others.

Jesus knew and understood the difficulty sanctified vessels will face, and therefore He took the time to pray for us.

Sanctify them by Your truth. Your word is truth. [18]*As You sent Me into the world, I also have sent them into the world.* [19]*And for their sakes I sanctify Myself, that they also may be sanctified by the truth.* (John 17: 17-19, NKJV).

Friends I think that you will agree with me that it was not an ordinary prayer; He prayed for His church!

Jesus prayed for you and me!

Today you and I are a part of that church!

Let's love like Christ does and extend the free gift of salvation to those who need a Savior!

Praise God His grace is still open to all!

William Layton Nelson, August 1, 2004.

EPILOGUE

Now that we have come to the ending of this book, I wonder if you found yourself going back over paths you have already taken; maybe roads on which you have traveled before?

Regardless of where we are in our journey of life, whether on roads well-trodden before or a new path, remember to thank God for walking ahead and beside you every step of the way.

As we journey back to days of long ago, there will be unwanted bitter memories, but let's remember that each experience and circumstance is exposure to His loving kindness and compassion. I must admit that some memories haunted me, but I am happy that I am a recipient of His grace.

I humbly accepted His grace, and the journey back has helped me to reprioritize, love and forgive as He does. Now if you are not where you think you should be at this time; my prayer is that you will take some time and journey toward the valley of hope where Jesus is waiting.

William Layton Nelson, 2021.

ABOUT THE AUTHOR

On March 3, 1945, in Providence St. James, Jamaica, William Layton Nelson was born to a happy couple, Zephaniah and Ethel Nelson. At the age of twelve, William discovered his love for poetry and songs; and as inspired, he has written more than seven hundred songs, poems, and devotionals which he considers to be attributes and gifts from God. He has compiled a great number of his writings into four other books. William attributes his love for God and worship to his parents who have never gone a day without morning and evening family devotions.

In the 1970s, William performed with the group, The Pleiades. Some of his lyrics were used to compile the gospel album, *Thunder and Lightning,* which brought spiritual upliftment and encouragement to many, and is available at https://www.ipromisegod.com and by other means - free downloads are available. William's poems are also available at: http://www.thestarlitecafe.com/poems/105/poem_91107362.htm

Printed in the United States
by Baker & Taylor Publisher Services